Overflow:

Tales of Butch-Femme Love, Sex, and Desire

By

Miel Rose

Earlier versions of some of these stories were previously published. *Undone* in *Best Lesbian Erotica 2008* edited by Tristan Taormino (Cleis Press, 2008). *All the Flood Gates Ever Made* in *Best Women's Erotica 2008* edited by Violet Blue (Cleis Press, 2008). *Overflow* in *Best Lesbian Love Stories 2009* edited by Simone Thorne (Alyson Books, 2008). *Love Letter* in *Ultimate Lesbian Erotica 2009* edited by Nicole Foster (Alyson Books, 2009). *Shopping* in *Surprise* edited by Tinder James (Racy Pages, 2010). *August Crazies* in *Lesbian Lust* edited by Sacchi Green (Cleis Press, 2010). *Rock Palace* in *Best Lesbian Romance 2011* edited by Radclyffe (Cleis Press, 2011). *Farmhand* in *The Harder She Comes* edited by D.L. King (Cleis, 2012). *The Suitor* in *Leather Ever After* edited by Sassafras Lowrey (Ravenous Romance, 2013)

2

Table of Contents

Intro

I started writing smut because I love to read smut. I have always been an avid and empathic reader and I love being swept up in the heat of a dirty story. Cheeks flushed, heart rate elevated, panties wet; I don't read erotica for titillation alone. I read it to get off.

But I ran into a conundrum when I first began exploring the world of smut/erotica. On the one hand, smut like Penthouse Letters with it's clear underlying power dynamics and stark language made me come really fast, but I was jerking off to mainstream, straight sex that was nothing like the sex I wanted to be having. Or, at least, not with men.

On the other hand, most lesbian erotica I came into contact with was so full of euphemism I found it profoundly not sexy. Sometimes the stories had a strong romantic component that would hooked me, but for the most part I wasn't interested in the sex the characters were having. These stories were also primarily about lesbians whose lives looked nothing like mine.

The exceptions to this was lesbian BDSM and old school butch/femme erotica, smut that I gravitated toward long before I realized I was wired that way. Here I found characters that I could relate to, language that made me come, and often a strong romance that tugged at my heart.

But there was so little of it out there!

My motivation became one shared by many other passionate writers; to write the stories I wanted to see in the world. Stories that reflect my desire for both romance and filthy, filthy smut. Stories that don't get told very often; about rural, working class, kinky, fat, emotionally active, wounded butches and femmes who love, fuck, and heal hard. I want to add to the voices that have told these stories before me, those working to tell them now, and those who will go on to tell them in the future.

This collection of stories spans 7 years of writing. Each story is fictitious, but contains reflections of my real live desires, hopes, challenges, and quest for growth. I hope you can find something to relate to, something that gets you hot, or at the least an inspiration to write your own stories.

Much love,

Miel Rose
December 30, 2012

Farmhand

The road was a piece of shit and their driveway was worse. I had taken the left where the directions said, and the driveway turned out to be another mile of bumpy ride worse than the near constant washboard of the main road. My truck was old and the shocks were not what they used to be. I was grinding the enamel off my teeth and wondering if anyone could possibly live out here when I turned a bend and saw the homestead.

I had answered an ad: "Queer couple seeks farmhand to help out in exchange for rent. Must have prior experience with gardening and goats."

I found it in the personals section of the local paper, which would have been weird, except for the fact that most of the women seeking women in this paper were looking for non-sexual relationships. I still looked every week though, hoping for something along the lines of "high femme top seeks butch service bottom with strong tongue."

I was at some kind of cross roads any way you looked at it. Between lovers, between jobs, couch surfing at a friend's. I had been looking for a way to get out of town and this seemed like the golden ticket.

I called the number and spoke to Taylor, told her about growing up rural with big gardens and my experiences on some CSA's outside the city. We set up an interview for me to see the place. Which was why I had driven down that crazy-ass dirt road.

I got out of the truck to look around. The house was beautiful, one of those gorgeous old New England farmhouses that you know are freezing in the winter. The yard was a jungle, tall grass mixed with flowers that had probably been an intentional garden once. I walked around the house and found an herb garden in better order, a chicken coup, vegetable gardens in various stages of cultivation, and the goat barn and pasture stretching out into the distance.

I was walking around the house, figuring I'd get to some kind of door eventually, when I heard noises coming from a window in front of me. Blood rushed to my cheeks. I thought, *it would have to be some kind of antique bed frame to make that kind of racket*. As I neared the window the sounds became distinct, the squeak of springs, whimpers, groans, and the slap of skin hitting skin.

I kept walking like I was on autopilot. I don't know what I was thinking. I don't make it a habit of spying on people through their windows, I swear. I kept walking, barely breathing, and peeked through the window past the white curtains.

The bed was in the corner of the room across from the window. On the bed was a beautiful naked woman on her knees, her hands gripping the old, squeaky frame. My eyes were drawn to her large breasts, shaking from the fucking she was getting. She had long brown hair, messy and tangled, and a luscious body that quivered and shook as the square hands on her hips pulled her into each thrust.

I ripped my eyes away from her body to get a look at her partner. This was Taylor, I guessed. She was really handsome, and definitely butch. I had a brief moment feeling the strangeness of reading someone's gender while watching them naked and fucking. I had the feeling that I would recognize this person's gender blindfolded. It wasn't her short, dark hair, or the fact that she was wearing the cock, fucking this beautiful woman from behind so hard you could hear their bodies slapping together. It was one of those things about gender that you can't put your finger on no matter how much you theorize and debate. It's something you know in your gut. I watched her lean over her lover's back and sink her teeth into the flesh of her shoulder. The luscious woman, Lilly, I guessed, screamed and arched her back, grinding her ass back at Taylor. Taylor reached around Lilly's body, found her clit and rubbed at it, making her convulse.

That broke the spell. I pulled my eyes away and continued around the house.

I sat down in the back of my truck, took a deep breath and counted to one hundred. They might still be in bed, but our appointment was for half an hour ago, so I went to their front door and knocked real loud. I felt shaky and nervous, not to mention horny as hell. My briefs were sticking to my crotch in a not so comfortable way. I was still blushing when Taylor opened the front door.

She had put on jeans and a t-shirt. Her breasts were bound under her shirt and I realized that I didn't know if Taylor identified as a woman. I was feeling really disoriented and tried desperately to get my mental footing.

"Hey, you must be Jess! Come on in, we're running late this morning." I tried to smile as I let myself be ushered into the house. "I'm Taylor, by the way." She held out her hand and I shook it, remembering her fingers rubbing Lilly's pussy moments earlier. I wondered if she had bothered to wash her hands.

"Beautiful place you got here." I said, looking around and trying to feel less awkward.

"Oh, thanks. I inherited it from my grandma when she passed. Me and Lilly have done a lot of work on it." She looked around as she said this, beaming with pride. She led me into the kitchen and opened the refrigerator. "Lilly's getting dressed. We were thinking we could make some lunch, then give you the major tour."

"That sounds great." I said, just as Lilly skipped in.

She had braided her hair into two messy braids, which she flung over her shoulders as she came in. She was smiling radiantly, beaming at me in the most disarming way. My knees got weak as she made her way toward me, her body as sexy clothed as it had been laid out naked on the bed. She bounced as she walked, making her hips and breasts shake. I could tell she felt good inside her body and it made me want to feel good inside her body too.

"HI! You must be Jess! I'm Lilly." She extended a slim, calloused hand. "Welcome. Did Taylor tell you that we're both starving and need to make some food? Are you hungry?"

We were standing in a close triangle and I was reeling from their energy, the heat and smells radiating from their bodies.

"Baby, I think we're overwhelming Jess. Hey, if you don't mind me asking, what pronoun do you prefer?" As Taylor asked this, Lilly was reaching above my head for a colander and I got a good view of the tops of her breasts pushing out over the bra she was wearing under her tank top.

"Umm, oh, yeah, I use female pronouns," I stammered. "And you?"

"Same, female. I used to identify more as male when I was younger, but I'm finding that shifts as I age. I identify more as a butch dyke now, as unpopular as that is these days."

This made Lilly giggle and Taylor grabbed her and kissed her neck. "And Miss Femme Princess here also uses female pronouns, but she can tell you how she ID's herself."

Lilly wiggled out of Taylor's arms, muttering. "Femme princess, my ass," and then louder, "I'm going to get some greens for salad." She strode out the door and I watched her ass sway from side to side before I realized I was staring. I looked at Taylor, hoping she hadn't caught me looking, and saw her watching Lilly too, absorbed in her own appreciation.

She shook her head and turned to me, smiling, and said, "Lets go get the eggs. I promised Lilly I'd make soufflé."

Living with Lilly and Taylor was awkward. I felt intimidated by their confidence, the sense of belonging they both exuded. They had some basic contentment going on that should have been a birthright, but most people I knew had missed it.

Then there was the fact that I seemed to get hard every time I was in the same room with either one of them. I thought this would pass as I got used to their company, but if anything it got worse.

At night, I could hear their sex loud from my room. I would create pictures in my head to match the noises coming from their bedroom. Lilly did not take it quietly. I would rub my clit fast and furious, thinking of Taylor fucking her or eating her pussy while they moaned and banged away on that old squeaky bed frame. I imagined myself in Taylor's place, laid out on top of Lilly's delicious body, fucking her deep with my cock. Sometimes, though I shied away from the thought during daylight hours, I would imagine myself in Lilly's position, getting plowed viciously by Taylor, getting fucked so hard my teeth rattled. Five seconds of these thoughts and I was screaming my come into my pillow.

I had always been attracted to femmes, especially tough-ass

femmes who could beat the shit out of me if they wanted, or would if I asked nicely. It was something familiar, something I knew. I had never been comfortable with my attraction to other butches though, never felt safe around it. I would occasionally have drunken sex with a buddy, but considered myself lucky if we could meet each other's eyes the next morning.

It complicated things that I grew to look up to Taylor so much. It's a funny thing not knowing if you want to be someone or fuck them, and knowing you definitely want to fuck their wife. By no means did I have it figured out by the time I started sleeping with them.

It happened with Lilly first.

She and Taylor had planned a trip into town. Lilly came into the kitchen that morning decked out in this sexy little gingham sundress, high-heeled sandals and full make-up. She didn't go into town that often and though she definitely presented femme around the farm, I had never seen her dress up like that before. I admit I blushed and looked away real quick. When they left, Lilly kissed me on the cheek, leaving a trace of her lipstick, and told me to be good.

I spent the morning doing my chores, stretching out the tension building in my body. I was constantly aware of how hard I was, and by lunchtime I was throbbing.

After eating I went into my room and took out my harness, my biggest cock, and my favorite porno. As much as I liked living with Lilly and Taylor, keeping my libido in check was starting to get strenuous.

I went into the living room and popped the porno into the VCR. It was an indie production I'd bought on sale and I liked it because the women had bigger, realistic bodies, and they seemed to enjoy getting fucked more than in other porn I've seen.

The movie opened with this beautiful woman, a voluptuous brunette sitting at her desk typing. She was a secretary and was about to be seduced and fucked by her boss. It was clichéd, sure, but it's the kind of shit that gets me off every time.

I reached under my cock and got as much cunt juice on my hand as possible. I ran my hand down my cock and the wet slickness against the give of the silicone made the hair stand up on my arms. The beautiful girl on the screen knelt down and took her boss's dick all the way into her mouth, her eyes bulging as her lips stretched around the base.

I closed my eyes and imagined Lilly kneeling in front of me, taking my cock between her red lips. My hand moved faster on my dick and I slid my other hand around, slipping two fingers up my cunt.

I opened my eyes and the brunette was still blowing her boss. He had taken her tits out of her blouse and was playing with them as she sucked him. He squeezed her nipples and she moaned loud around his cock. I closed my eyes again and thought of Lilly's gorgeous tits. I remembered the first time I saw her, Taylor fucking her so hard from behind that her tits bounced up and slapped down against her torso. I groaned and moved my fingers faster in and out of my cunt.

Then, above the TV sex noises, I heard the screen door bang shut and the click of heels on the wood floor.

My eyes flew open and there she was in all her gingham sundressed glory, standing in the doorway with her hand on her beautiful hip. It happened that fast.

"I told you to be good," she said, tilting her head and looking me up and down. Then she looked over at the TV screen where the brunette was straddling the now-seated boss's lap and bouncing up and down on his cock. "Nice." Lilly said, and walked towards me.

"Hey, Lilly, I'm really sorry you found me like this." I stammered as I tried to collect myself and stand up.

"Yeah, I bet you're sorry." she said, and pushed me back down on the couch.

She was right where I'd imagined her minutes earlier, on her knees in front of my cock.

"My, what a big boy you are," she purred. She looked me right in the eye, raised her hand level with the head of my cock, and flicked it. She actually flicked it. Then she said, "You think you can work this monster?"

This challenge made my clit rock hard under my cock. This woman was my wettest dream. She was also married, for all intents and purposes, so what was she doing between my legs, smirking at my cock?

"Lilly? What's going on? What about-" She shushed me, crawled up my body and wrapped her fingers around my throat.

"I know you want me," she said, squirming in a way that made my body feel like it was dissolving into the couch. "I see how you watch me." She nuzzled her face into my neck and licked her wicked tongue across my jugular vein. "I bet you think about me when you touch yourself."

"Ohh, fuck, Lilly, what are you doing to me?"

"Exactly what you want me to do, sugar." She kissed me full on the mouth, slipping her tongue between my lips. She tasted so good I groaned into her mouth.

14

Breaking the kiss, she said, "Hands behind your head, now." It was an abrupt order, but I complied with speed. "Good boy," she said, leaning forward to run her tongue over my bottom lip.

"Fuck," she said, standing up, "I'm so fucking wet." She slipped her panties down her legs and threw them into the corner. Pulling her dress up around her waist she said, "See what you did to me, Jess?"

Her pussy hair was trimmed short and her clit was so swollen it stuck straight out between her puffy cunt lips. I wanted her so bad.

"Oh, God, I want to taste you. Let me suck you, Lilly, please? Let me touch you. I'll do anything, please."

"Maybe next time. Take off your cock."

"What?!"

"Boy, I know you heard me," she said in her no nonsense voice.

Wondering what she was after, I brought my hands to the buckle of my harness.

"Hand it to me," she said, and trembling inside, I did.

She stepped into the leg straps and adjusted the harness to fit her luscious body. Call me dense, but that was when it hit me that she intended to fuck me with my own cock. My cunt got wetter than it'd been in years.

"Mmm, it feels good to wear a cock again," she said, jutting her hips forward and staring down at it. "Now, lay down on the couch and spread your legs for me."

I did as she said. I wanted to be good for her, to please her however I could, and to be honest, I desperately wanted that cock inside me.

She crawled onto the couch between my legs and spread them farther apart. She ran her thumb up my slit, moaned, and put the cock head at the mouth of my cunt.

She pushed into me and leaned forward to kiss me. I felt a fullness expand inside me that got bigger as she started to fuck me.

Her teeth sank into my bottom lip. She moaned into my mouth and fucked me harder. She was as loud fucking as she was getting fucked, and her noises were all *girl*, a constant reminder that this was a femme fucking me.

As I got closer she got louder, saying, "Come on sweet boy, come for me. Come for me before I come up inside you." She rotated her hips, twisting the cock inside me and I went off like fucking dynamite, coming hard around the thick base of her cock.

Things got weird after that. I could tell she wanted to talk, but I panicked and ran, hid out in my room for the rest of the day, playing music loud, pretending I couldn't hear her knocking. I heard Taylor drive up around dark and wondered where the hell she'd been, and why Lilly had come home early without her.

I skulked into the kitchen the next day and Taylor was waiting for me.

"Grab your sleeping bag, I want to take you someplace." she said, and lugged a couple heavy-looking bags out to her truck.

I have to admit I was scared shitless, but Taylor had always been kind to me and a part of me trusted her more than I should have, knowing her such a short time. I followed her out to the truck and we rode in excruciating silence for 35 miles.

The hike was short, the bags were heavy, and we were

sweating like pigs by the time we reached the spot she was looking for.

"This land belongs to my uncle, but he never comes here anymore." It was the first thing she'd said since the kitchen. Then, just like that she launched into it, "Lilly feels real bad about yesterday. She should have just come out and told you that we'd talked about you two having sex, that I'm ok with it. Our relationship is pretty defined and she doesn't get to express top energy very often, I think she got a little carried away."

My mouth hung open. Whatever I had been expecting, this wasn't it.

"So," Taylor continued, "in an effort not to repeat her mistake, I'd like to make it known that we've also discussed how much I'd like to fuck you. If you're not interested, it's cool. We can still sit down and negotiate something between you and Lilly. I know it could get messy, but I'm willing to give it a try, see if it works."

Taylor looked down at her hands while she talked and it occurred to me that even a confidant person fears rejection. I could find no way past the lump in my throat to speak, so I simply reached for her hand and drew her towards me.

Her eyes locked on mine and she said, "Are you sure?"

I swallowed, cleared my throat, and said, "I'm sure."

Then her mouth was on mine. Taylor slid her tongue into my mouth, then sucked my tongue into hers. She broke the kiss to arrange the pile of sleeping bags on the ground and pushed me back onto them. Climbing on top of me, she wedge her thigh hard between my legs and continued the kiss, sucking my bottom lip, sliding down to my neck and sinking her teeth into me.

"You are so fucking hot, Jess." Her hands found my nipples

hard and she pinched them, twisting. "Why don't you take your shirt off for me?"

I wriggled out of my T-shirt, exposing my chest to her. The heat and wet of her mouth on my tits made me crazy. She devoured me, sucking as much of my flesh into her mouth as would fit. I thrust my hips against her thigh and her hand snaked down to my crotch, cupping me over my jeans. She unzipped my pants and I helped her pull them down along with my underwear.

She grinned at me, reached into her back pocket and pulled out a glove. "Always be prepared," she said. Her gloved hand found my cunt wet and swollen. She plunged into me and I yelped, surprised at how sore I was.

Taylor pulled out gently and I said, embarrassed, "Sorry, I guess I'm a little sore from yesterday. It's been awhile…"

She grinned at me. "Yeah, Lilly said that was a monster you were strapping." Her fingers pressed against my perineum and slid past to my asshole. "How about this?" she asked as she circled my hole with her fingers.

"Ohhh, god," I said, and rocked my hips into her.

She reached into the nearest pack, pulled out a bottle of lube and squirted some onto her glove. It must be some kind of natural law that lube is always cold at first, even on hot days. I felt my ass clench around the tip of her finger at the shock of it. Her teeth locked around my nipple and a noise I didn't recognize as my own escaped my throat. She slid another finger up inside me and started fucking me with short, hard thrusts, her fingers pushed in as far as they could go. Her hand hit my perineum with each stroke, sending dull hammer blows of pleasure along my nerves.

I got lost in the conflict of feeling, her sharp wolf teeth chewing my nipples, the dull thud of her fingers fucking me, the fullness in my ass as she slid a third finger inside me. Every sensation seemed to be set on overwhelming me with its intensity. I never wanted it to end and simultaneously prayed to come, fearing I might burst some organ with all that pressure building inside.

She looked me in the eye and said, "Why don't you rub that clit for me? It looks ready to explode."

My hand flew to my clit and started stroking with a hard, vicious intensity. I watched Taylor's face as she watched me rub my cunt, and that alone could have pushed me over. But I also had her fingers pounding my asshole, her other hand putting increasing pressure on my wind pipe, her filthy whispers in my ear telling me to come.

And I did, with those earthquake spasms that orgasms are made of when you have fingers buried deep in your ass. I shook so hard she had to hold me down in case I flopped away from her.

It has never stopped being strange to me, that space after you come, after the beast of lust falls asleep and you are lying there with another person who has just watched you double over in orgasmic spasms, shrieking like a maniac. Someone who has played an instrumental role in your orgasm, seen you vulnerable outside of your shell, felt your slick and swollen internals.

I expected the worst. It's a bad habit, but easy to pick up in this world.

Taylor was a master at making me comfortable, though. It's a crazy shock to see tenderness where you look for disgust. It's a shock to find yourself 15 minutes later, still naked, wrestling the fully clothed person who just fucked your ass.   To be so engrossed telling your life story to this person, so caught up in the feeling of their arms around you that you don't even realize it's getting late until the beauty of the sunset registers in your brain.

We collected our things and I thought about what I'd been up to in the last two days.   Where would this bring me, fucking my housemates and semi-employers?   I wondered what it would be like walking into the house and seeing Lilly, knowing she knew what I'd been doing with her lover all day.   I wondered how I would feel going to bed alone knowing they would have each other, like always.   I wondered where and how I could fit into this equation, and if it would prove too difficult for someone like me who only took freshman algebra.

I wondered and worried a lot on our way back, and I came to a place for the first time in my life where making the decision to stop worrying seemed like a possibility.   I had always been a chronic borrower of trouble and it had kept me out of a whole lot of bad situations, but a lot of good ones too.

Sitting in Taylor's truck on the drive home, I made the decision to take things as they came.   If Lilly and Taylor got sick of me, kicked me out, broke my heart, well, as my grandpa used to say, I would burn that bridge when I came to it.

Overflow

My heart is too easily influenced. I figure this is why loud, fast bass beats give me heart palpitations and why I can't enjoy a casual fuck to save my life.

The issue translates well to Chinese medicine and I work on it with my acupuncturist. She treats the defensive perimeter, the heart's protection that needs strengthening. For this, needles and moxa on the pericardium channel are indicated.   But still, there is the build-up that inevitably happens despite the perimeter, and the safety check valve that keeps my heart from getting too full. When this overflows I can't stop laughing or crying and my armpits smell like burnt coffee. Heart channel overflow, a disorder of an excess nature.

Excess sorrow, excess joy. My friend tells me a sad story and I can't stop crying for hours. My roommate has a new date and I'm high on the second hand smoke from the fires of her romance. Reading the newspaper is totally out of the question.

Sometimes it's called empathy, sometimes bi-polar disorder or manic depression. You're either crazy or just too fucking sensitive. I can be a real rollercoaster.

The summer I fell for Tarn, my trickling stream of heart overflow turned swollen like floodwater. I was so quick to laugh or cry it left the people around me dizzy, and no one could ever really be sure what I was feeling from those signifiers. I might have felt insecure about this, but to be honest I was so busy falling crazy in love with her I didn't think about it much. And fuck, she must have had it bad for me too, because I was a real lunatic that summer.

Tarn was the kind of guy who stopped wearing girl's underwear when she was three years old. The kind that will show you little kid pictures of themselves clad only in trunks at the local swimming hole and make you think, "What a sweet, precious little boy you were."

She was named after a body of water that defies the expectations of gravity, and as any fantasy paperback will tell you, there is a special magic in how you name a thing. She was lucky to have parents who gave into her willfulness, who threw their hands up in exasperation instead of beating her black and blue. She came into this world knowing exactly who she was and she stuck to her plastic cowboy guns around the issue no matter how much crazy shit she got growing up.

I also came into this world knowing who I was gender-wise, but the issue of my gender was confused by the fact that it somewhat approximated people's expectations of what I was supposed to be. There is the side of that which means I rarely got the kind of shit gender variant queers get growing up, and there is the side that is all about isolated lonely confusion, trying to fit a round peg in a square hole, all about nothing in my world giving a name for what I was. It was obvious I was a girl and everyone said I would like boys.

This turned out to be true to some extent, if you ignore the fact that I only like boys with the same plumbing as me.

The summer I met Tarn I was trying to make peace between my extremes, to find some balance. My mode of operation was to recognize the blessing and the curse of every situation. I was all about the unification of opposites, like holding two beasts in the same space and keeping them from ripping each other's throats out.

Tarn and me weren't exactly opposites; we were so alike in some ways it was spooky. It was like we mirrored parts of each other, looking glass style, backwards. Like we had the same basic elements, but had chosen different ways to get to where we were going. The effect was sometimes disorienting, but overall joyful.

"We complement each other perfectly," I said to her on one of our early dates.

She laughed. "Like red wine and steak?" she asked, her lips pressed against the skin below my jaw, her hand creeping up my skirt.

We were picnicking in the graveyard and it reminded me of earlier days. "Like a 40 of malt liquor on an empty stomach when you're 16 and it's your first punk rock summer."

Her head tilted back and she laughed loud, from her guts. I felt immensely pleased with myself, a pride all out of proportion.

"Baby, are you saying our relationship makes you feel like vomiting for hours?" Her lips were back on my neck, her teeth grazing my skin, her hand further up my skirt, fingertips brushing my panty line.

"Ohh, how can I think when you're doing that to me?"

"What do you need to think for?" She pushed my back flat to the blanket and my legs spread open on well-oiled hinges.

It was dusk and we were in an old part of the cemetery. People didn't come here to mourn anymore; they came here to drink or do drugs or fuck, or sometimes to study the old and beautiful gravestones. The graveyard was so old that I knew whoever was buried underneath me had long ago decomposed into earth, so old it was before formaldehyde and concrete started fighting to keep every human body immortal.

I felt Tarn's weight settle between my legs and my bones shifted to accommodate her. My legs wrapped around her hips and my arms pulled her close.

I hadn't been fucked in a graveyard since the fore mentioned punk rock summer of my 16th year, but this seemed to be her plan. My anxiety built at the thought of discovery, but Tarn between my legs quickly demanded all my attention.

She rocked her hips, pressing down on my cunt, and kissed me in that amazingly gentle way she used to thoroughly posses my mouth. Those kisses left no room in my perception for anything but heat and wet and the softness of mucus membranes touching. Her tongue was in my mouth and it was filling my whole world. I moaned into that cavity and ground my pussy against the denim covering her pelvis. She reached her hands under the sides of my skirt, slid them along my hips. Her mouth left mine and her teeth closed on my earlobe.

"I want your ass. Roll over," she growled.

My body did not want her weight gone, but she raised herself up before I could protest and flipped me over onto my stomach. I lifted my ass in the air for her and felt her hands peeling my panties away from my body.

The smell of cut grass was in my nose and a breeze blowing past brought out goose bumps along my skin, rustled the leaves on the oak above us. Nothing in my environment helped me to ignore that I was outside and visible despite the dying light.

It was a contest between anxiety and desire until I felt her tongue slip between my pussy lips and her nose press against my asshole.

"Mmm, you're so wet," she said, before sticking her tongue up my cunt.

Her hands gripped my ass cheeks, squeezing them hard. Her tongue left my pussy and traveled up to my asshole, lapped at the center.

I could feel my heart swelling up and I caught a whiff of burnt coffee from under my arm. Something was building to be released, something besides the orgasm building in my cunt. I wanted this tension released from my body, knew that the overflow would happen inevitably, but that if I helped it out the results would be way more rewarding.

Tarn was tongue fucking my ass and this was hard to interrupt. Between my moans I managed to whisper, "Tarn, baby, I need you to hurt me. Please?"

She groaned into my ass and I felt her teeth on my ass cheek, pain shooting up my back. "What do you want, darlin'? Tell me what you want."

"Spank me? Will you baby?"

At this point in our relationship, Tarn had never spanked me. Our sex was rough from the start, but somehow I hadn't gotten around to asking her for this. I felt myself fall towards bottom space, feeling shy and hoping I was safe with her.

"Get up and take your shirt off."

I felt my ears turn hot like coals, but did as she said, shivering as her hands slid the cups of my bra off my tits. Her fingers pinched my nipples hard. This made every nerve in my breasts stand out like a glow-in-the-dark map in my mind, like when light shines in your eyes a certain way and you get a flash of the veinous structure of your own eyeball.

"Lean up against the stone."

It was a large and heavy gravestone, so worn and lichen covered it had been hard to read the inscription earlier in the daylight. The granite was rough against my tits, scraping my nipples as she positioned me. Her hands went to my hips, her crotch rubbing against me, humping me from behind. She leaned over and kissed my neck so sweet the muscles in my lower back clenched up.

"I'm going to beat your ass so hard. You ready girl?"

Her hand came down with force and the noise it made seemed way too loud for the wide, dark space we were in. The pain registered along my nerves and my hips bucked, wanting more.

"Yes, thank you, thank you baby. Please? Please, more?" My face heated in shadow, embarrassed at the begging automatically spilling from my mouth.

I sensed her hand go back, felt the displacement of air as it sped towards me, felt my body tense for it, and then felt her hand stop just short of my skin. The tease was effective, my body shivered with anticipation and I couldn't help whining, "Please, Tarn, please! I need you!"

Her hand was on me fast, a series of sharp sounds splitting the night, hard palm hitting soft skin.

The first stage of spanking arousal had me panting, mouth open, moaning as I backed my ass into her strokes. My body felt like one giant pulse, all heart and clit and the enormous pressure of blood. I felt that space open up underneath my heart, full with relief and love, some overwhelming and indefinable mix of emotion, the way it does when there is something you've needed for so long and you're finally getting it. Her hand slammed into my ass, a fast and hard rhythm, one I'd been missing.

Stage two had me shying away from her hits. This was when the initial relief of pain started wearing off, when the pain formed an edge, became sharp instead of diffuse. When I started questioning the sanity of what I craved and begged for. My hips started twisting from side to side, tying to evade her palm. A pointless impulse, but hard to control. Tarn knew me well enough by then to expect some verbal indication that I wanted to stop.

And I didn't. She was whaling on me and it fucking hurt, but every stroke brought me closer to stage three, where all the jagged edges smooth out and each hit makes me feel like I could come.

I froze and stayed as still as I could for her. We were making fire between us and it danced from her hands along the surface of my skin. I felt my heart swelling big, felt her palms connecting dots between my nerve clusters, drawing a map of pain on my surface.

WHACK! Her hand came down lower than she had been spanking me, hitting my parted thighs and making a sticky sound on impact. It felt so good on my pussy lips that I inched my knees apart and angled my hips to give her better access. Tarn took the hint and aimed her slap between my thighs. She groaned and rubbed the sting away, her whole hand kneading my sloppy cunt, before smacking me again.

My pussy lips burned and I wanted her inside me with a sudden and overwhelming passion.

"Tarn," I gasped between hits. "Tarn, don't stop baby, just listen."

"Tell me, love, I'm all ears." Her breathing was as heavy as her hand spanking me into the gravestone.

"Fuck me, baby, please? Don't stop hitting me, but I need you inside me, now!"

The guy can follow directions. Her fingers were inside me before I finished my sentence, plunging into my overflow, stretching me in the best way. Her hand pulsed with heat and the buzz of all that kinetic energy, thrusting into my pussy, fingertips separating liquids from solids.

Her left hand slapped down on my cheek, adding sting to the heaven building in my pussy. She gave me a couple of good whacks, the pain a sweet contrast to her fingers pounding at my insides.

It was awkward though, the guy not being left handed, and I wanted her closer, wanted her covering me with as much of her body as possible. I wanted her thrusting into me, fucking me with all of her.

"Come here," I said, looking over my shoulder at her through the darkness. "Come here, baby."

I felt her chest on my back, felt her thick fingers pump deep inside me backed by the thrust of her hips, felt her left arm wrap around my neck and press my windpipe. Her heavy breath was right up close to my ear, sending shivers down my spine as she whispered, "Like this, you little slut? Is this what you want?"

The denim of her jeans rubbed against my sensitive, freshly beaten skin. Her pelvis rocked her hand into my pussy hard and fast, riding me good as her teeth chewed at my neck. She moaned into my ear and I could tell that her clit was big and swollen inside her jeans, rubbing against the heel of her hand through layers of cloth.

I knew she would come; she's talented that way. It takes me a lot longer, with more direct stimulation, although I've been known to come dry humping her cock every now and then.

Her bicep flexed, putting pressure on my windpipe, making it hard to breathe. She was tongue fucking my ear, slow and deliberate, and groaning with each hard thrust, all of which made my back so ticklish I thought my muscles would seize up any second.

My cunt was all fire and water, burning and sloppy wet. Her fingers drummed against the roof of my pussy and I was getting light headed from lack of air and the overwhelming feeling that if I didn't come soon I might explode.

Tarn shifted her hand, her knuckles finding a new and glorious place inside me. Her hips started thrusting faster, driving her fingers deeper into my pussy, and I could tell she was close, so close. I rocked my hips back at her with all my might and slipped my hand between my legs.

Sometimes finding the key to my own orgasm is like some crazy drawn out storybook quest. Sometimes it wouldn't matter if the most talented dyke Casanova was fucking me, using all the fancy toys from her magic bag of tricks, painting the raunchiest porno in my head with her filthy mouth growling close to my ear. Sometimes its like the fail-safe fails and my overflow can't find a way out.

And sometimes Tarn fucks me so hard and deep, I rub my clit fast and furious, she groans her come loud in my ear and it's like dynamite to that dam inside me. I'm gushing come all over her pants, sobbing and laughing and holding on tight as she kisses my face over and over, cuddling me in the dark above the remains of somebody's ancestor.

Or at least that's how it was that night.

I lay there with Tarn, staring up at the stars, letting all of my overflow seep into hallowed ground.

All the Floodgates Ever Made

The herb garden was big, but I was almost done with the job. It had taken me more than a week to get it in order. It was a dream working in such an old and diverse herb garden. There were huge, beautiful stands of Lavender, Wormwood and Rosemary, decades old, and I grew intoxicated surrounded by their strong fragrances. There were Poppies gone to seed, their pods rattling, broadcasting seed all over the garden. Come spring they would be everywhere, along with the Angelica and the Calendula. Besides the old European standbys, Mrs. O'Connelly had transplanted a dozen or more natives from the surrounding woods and trained them to cultivation. There was Doll's Eyes with its white berries, each one with a black spot on the top looking like tiny eyeballs, and its cousin Black Cohosh. There was the shiny ground cover of Partridge Berry, the lacy foliage of Bleeding Heart, the shocking blue berries of Clintonia. Being a plant lover and an herb nerd, I was head over heels.

I was finishing weeding between the Mugwort and the Greater Celendine, and with a last tug at a Dandelion root who had strayed from the area allowed to the Taraxacums, I sighed and got up to bring my pile of weeds to the compost.

I'd been called in for this job because no one on Wade's crew knew enough about medicinal plants to handle the herb garden. They'd been hired to help out the elderly couple who lived on this old farmstead. Wade asked me if I'd be interested in weeding a garden that might have been made up entirely of weeds for all they knew about it. Some of the plants were indeed weeds, but interesting ones, and I could tell what was to stay and what was for the compost heap. So, since I was broke and jobless, I agreed to come out and whip the garden into shape.

Not that I didn't have my reservations. I make it a policy not to work jobs with people I'm dating. Plus, spending my days working with a bunch of macho dudes wasn't my idea of a good time, even if some of them are like my brothers.

Maybe an outsider would have no idea what I'm talking about, just seeing us as one big happy dyke work crew. The thing is, I'm a femme. While I have no qualms pulling on my overalls as practicality dictates, I still find myself with insecurities about how others perceive my gender when I'm in that mode. Most people's perceptions of gender are so shallow, skin deep indeed. Also, I wasn't looking forward to the typical scenario of having to prove I'm a capable and hard worker just because you mostly see me in a skirt. Borrowing trouble, per usual, working in the garden had been pleasant and solitary with little of the bullshit I had anticipated.

So, after dumping my weeds in the compost and hosing off my muddy hands, I went off towards the house to check the time. Passing the barn, I saw Wade, pitch fork in hand, walking towards the ladder to the loft. Her T-shirt was dark with sweat and her hair was sticking up in clumps. She turned and saw me, breaking into her crazy-ass grin that more often than not reduces my panties to wet land.

"Good, you finished with the garden just in time to help me pitch the rest of this hay."

"Honey, you know pitching hay isn't in my job description," I said, hand on hip.

"Baby, it's easy. Come on, grab a pitch fork."

Sighing, I grabbed the fork and followed Wade up into the loft.

Truth be told, I was tired and I just wanted to go home and take a bath. But there wasn't much hay left, so I got to work pitching it off the loft. I worked steadily for about five minutes before I realized Wade had stopped and was grinning at me, leaning on her pitch fork. I was hot and sweaty and irritation was stronger than any sweet feelings I had for her.

"Don't fucking look at me."

"Why the fuck not?" Her smile did not falter and she threw her pitch fork into the hay.

"I'm here to work, not look sexy for you." I just wanted to get this job done, go home and get in the shower. I was starting to feel self conscious in my muddy overalls. I was used to being dressed up and ready for a date when I was around Wade, and as much as I wished my self-confidence was rock-hard and not related to my outfit, it was starting to crumble around the edges.

I stopped working and dropped my fork as Wade started walking towards me. Her eyes had gone flinty and her jaw was clenched, making her muscles stick out from her jawbone. When she reached me she didn't stop, but slowly pushed me backwards, helping me navigate the hay while giving me a look that sent icy chills down my spine. My back hit the wall and she grabbed my chin with her big, calloused hand.

In a deep, slow voice brimming with authority, she said, "I *know* you. Don't you *ever* forget that. I know exactly who you are." She chuckled without cracking the harshness of her expression. "Yeah, like you aren't just as femme in muddy overalls as you are in a skirt and heels."

I guess I was being pretty blatant in my insecurity, but I swear it felt like she was reading my mind.

She turned her head and spit onto the dusty floor of the loft. "That's fucking bullshit. I love that you're a hard worker." Her grin was back, softening the angles of her face, but not quite reaching her eyes. "In fact, watching you has got my dick hard. Too bad I don't have the balls to pack at work."

I felt tears filling my eyes. Her thumb caressed my cheek and her face became tender without losing its intensity. Leaning forward, she kissed me gently, slowly sliding her tongue into my mouth. My knees turned to water and I opened to her, my body relaxing against the barn wall. Her mouth turned to my neck, at first kissing my skin softly with parted, moist lips until I was squirming against her, and then more urgently, using enough suction and teeth to leave me swollen and bruised. Her hand left my jaw and drifted under the bib of my overalls, lifting my tits up and rubbing my nipples in slow firm circles with her thumbs.

Her mouth moved up to my ear and her voice was husky as she said, "I'm going to fuck you."

The spell was broken and I balked. Maybe I could be a good bottom for her in the bedroom, but we were at work, and although no one could see us up here, they could certainly hear us.

"Wade, I don't want to end this job getting caught fucking in the O'Connelly's loft."

"Baby, relax, no one's going to miss us up here."

With a firm grip, she pivoted our bodies sideways and down onto the nearest pile of hay. Really, my cunt was wet and swollen already, and with Wade between my legs my protests were forgotten. Well, almost.

"What if I make too much noise?" I moaned, as she thrust her groin against my canvas-covered pussy.

"I'm not worried about it." She grabbed my arms and held them down above my head and kissed me hard. Then, shifting her grip with one hand holding my wrists, she moved her other hand between us and fumbled to unbutton my fly. A moan escaped my lips and I felt myself frowning, desperate to get fucked, but scared of the consequences. "Baby, relax," she crooned as she saw my face. "How's your pussy?" She slipped her hand through my fly and into my panties, finding my pussy soaking wet and desperate for her fingers. "Jesus Fucking Christ you're wet." Her eyes closed in rapture and she lowered her head to my chest as she plunged her fingers deep inside me.

I wanted to scream my head off, but instead babbled a stream of quiet pleadings, "Yes, yes, fuck me, fuck me. Harder baby, please? Harder? You feel so good baby, your fingers are so good, so good. Don't stop, don't stop."

Her grip tightened on my wrists and she groaned in my ear, saying, "Yeah baby, tell me you like it, that's right, give it to me." She raised her head and looked into my eyes and said, "I'm going to make you come."

Now, I don't come when I get fucked, and maybe it's like Wade says, it's because I'm scared and stop her before she brings me there. All I know is that there gets to be this point when what I'm feeling is so intense I can't tell if it's pleasure or pain and yeah, I guess I get scared. It's just too much. Well, up in that hayloft Wade was quickly taking me to that threshold and it became obvious she meant to push me over. She was gripping my wrists so tightly that I was losing circulation and she was looking deep in my eyes with so much intensity that I knew all I had to do was say the word and she would stop.

I didn't. My pussy felt like it was going to burst into flames from the friction going on inside me. I was so wet and she was fucking me so hard I could hear her fingers pounding in and out of me. That intense pressure was building and I was worried I was going to lose control, the feeling was so big. I was getting scared, but Wade just kept on fucking me relentlessly, like her arm wasn't about to fall off. She just kept going, fucking her fingers in and out of my wet, sopping pussy while this feeling built inside me, some huge wave set on breaking down all the floodgates ever made.

Wade's eyes were locked on mine and I was staring back in defiance, letting her know I was right there with her, daring her to push me a little further. And she did, her fucking becoming more focused, concentrated.

Her hand left my wrists and clamped down on my mouth right as I was about to start screaming. The wave of feeling broke and I felt like I was going to drown in it. This was not like the orgasms I was used to. My body seized up in a round of intense spasms, my pussy clamping down hard on her fingers.

"That's right, girl. Come for me, baby. Give it to me. You're doing so good. Just a little more, baby, give me a little more. Good girl, that's it." Wade's fingers kept stroking inside me, stretching out my orgasm, riding the waves. My hands, newly released, were holding Wade's hand clamped down over my mouth and I bit into her palm trying to keep this ungodly banshee wailing from leaving my mouth. I took a deep breath and whimpered against her palm, kissing the indentations left by my teeth. My muscles relaxed and Wade moved her fingers in slow circles against the walls of my cunt, making me jump and clamp down on her again.

I was so lost in the feeling that it took me a minute to realize I was soaking wet, more so than I had been minutes ago. It felt like I had ejaculated about a pint of come into my overalls. When my pussy finally stopped contracting, Wade pulled her fingers out of me. She gently ran them through my wetness and then stopped, her whole hand cupping me, holding my cunt. I pulled her hand off my mouth and lay there panting as she smoothed my bangs off my forehead, planting soft kisses all over my face and neck.

"How are you sweetheart?"

I pulled her down and curled into her. She was grinning, very pleased with herself, I'm sure. As I shifted I could feel that my come was soaking through my overalls. I groaned.

"Wade, it looks like I pissed myself! How am I going to say good-bye to the O'Connellys covered in come!"

"I don't know, sugar, but a far amount squirted out on me, so I guess we're in the same boat."

I looked, and indeed she had a patch of wet soaking the front of her shirt. How had I ejaculated so much without even realizing it? Still, we weren't exactly in the *same* boat. It didn't look like she pissed her pants.

"I have an idea," her eyes lit when she said it. "Come with me."

She pulled her hand out of my pants, stroking my throbbing clit once more, making me twitch, and kissed me. Standing up, she reached down to help me to my feet. My legs felt shaky and I buttoned the fly of my overalls as Wade walked to the edge of the loft and looked over. "The coast is clear," she said, grinning like crazy. "Lets go."

My eyes narrowed in suspicion. Whatever was making her smile like that, my intuition advised caution. But I followed her down the ladder and stood in one dark corner of the barn, waiting to see what madness she was up to. I was looking closely at the antique scythes hanging on the wall when I heard her turn on the hose and felt the frigid water hit me full blast.

"Ahh! Wade! I *hate* you!" My lungs seized up in shock at the cold and I gasped for breath. Turning around, I pushed her away hard, but not before she got the hose down the front of my overalls. "Ohh, *YOU*!!!" I got control of the hose and turned it on her, hitting her right in the face. She put up her hands, sputtering and called surrender.

"Okay! Okay! Stop!"

I know I had wanted a shower, but this was ridiculous. I turned off the hose, still furious, while she doubled over in hysterical laughter. Later I would admit that it was a good plan, but that didn't make me any less pissed, or my sensitive pussy any less cold. I threw the hose down, about to advance upon her when I looked up to see half our work crew and Mr. O'Connelly staring at us with open mouths. Well, there was always later. Wade would get what was coming to her.

So I said good-bye to my employers soaking from head to toe with indistinguishable wetness. All in all, it wasn't that bad a way to end a job.

Love Letter

You've been in my thoughts so much lately. Waking and sleeping, though most mornings I can't remember my dreams. When I wake up it's like you were just in bed with me, like maybe you're in the bathroom down the hall instead of an ex-lover I haven't seen for years. And when I leave my house for the day I keep mistaking people walking down the street for you. It's like you're hovering in my peripheral vision; if I turn my head fast enough maybe I'll catch you.

Where are you? I know it's a little late in the game, but you being on my mind so much brings up this idea of fate and how often we used to talk about destiny in relation to us. That was back when we were so crazy in love we couldn't walk straight. That time is so present with me now and I can't shake this idea that you're about to show up at my door any minute.

There's this old conversation of ours that keeps playing out in my head. I was going through a tough time then, kind of like now, which is probably why I'm thinking about it so much. Who knew your words would stay with me after all this time?

We were on a date and you were making me dinner and I was heart sore over some crazy kind of drama that only exists in small queer communities. I can't even remember the cause, but at the time it was triggering a whole lot of self-doubt. I felt so drained, like the slightest challenge could make me fold, make me question my strength.

I was trying to explain this to you when you grabbed my chin and looked fiercely into my eyes.

"Girl, you are so fucking strong, don't you ever doubt that. That's the crazy thing about you. Hell, that's the crazy thing about a lot of the femmes I've known. You're as strong as steel, like you could take on anything if you had to, and you have. I mean, you do. Somehow that steel doesn't form an edge and cut you inside. Somehow you can still be so open and so strong at the same time."

I gaped at you, shook my head, knowing you had it all wrong.

You said, "Baby, that's why I love you so goddamn much." You threw your hands up in exasperation, slapping them down on your thighs. "That's what gets me every time, your crazy strength and your vulnerability. I don't know, maybe you'll get pissed when I say this, but that's what makes me want to protect you so much. I've seen way too many people turn hard in my life. It's not like you can't take care of yourself, I *know* you can, but why should you always have to? I mean, fuck! Why should any of us always have to? Why do we do so much fighting alone? Baby, I just want you to know I got your back."

As I remember, it wasn't long after that you rolled me onto that back you wanted to protect, crawled between my legs, and fucked me so sweet for the rest of the night.

It was a continuing theme with us, this concept of how to protect each other in a world that wanted us broken or dead. I remember slow dancing with you in this bar, slow dancing even though we could have easily been grinding like everyone else on the floor. We were cheek to cheek, your hands on my hips, my lower back, my nails tracing patterns on your neck and shoulders. You whispered in my ear, asked me if I thought you were a misogynist pig. This was because 15 minutes earlier you had slammed some guy against the wall, your hand on his throat, because he had reached up my skirt when I was walking past. You asked me if I felt like you were trying to fight my fights for me, taking up too much space, being too macho. Your face was hot against mine. I wondered if you were thinking about all the bar fights you used to get into, growing up poor and angry and queer. How you were trying to calm down in your old age of 35 years.

Instead of answering you directly, I told you about the time I bitched out this woman I over heard saying how sorry she felt for masculine women, how twisted and wounded they must feel inside. A deep and terrible violence had welled up in me. I tried to stay calm, tried to tell her nicely that she didn't know shit. I wanted to spit in her face, beat her senseless. This was only partly in defense of you, of all of the butches and trans-masculine guys I've loved as friends, brothers, or lovers. It was also in defense of me, of my gendered, queer life. You are a piece of me. Not a half to fit mine and make a whole, I'm whole all on my own, but like a piece of my same puzzle. The puzzle that makes up our big, crazy, queer, homo lives. Sometimes fighting each other's fight is the same as fighting our own. Like you said, why should we always have to fight alone? Even if we are on different sides of this circle that makes up queer gender, this circle everyone tries to teach us is a straight line.

You being willing to fight for femmes, you trying so hard to stay on top of the misogyny that threatens to rip us and our community apart, this is what made me powerfully in love with you. The fact that you were the best lover I've ever had was icing on the cake. Mile high icing that just might have dissolved my teeth if I didn't brush right after.

Metaphor can't really describe it though, the way you could be so sweet and tender while you fucked me raw from behind, beating my ass until I bruised. The way you could cause me pain so sweet and overwhelming it would have me crying for hours, fighting demons I barely knew I had, until I emerged feeling light, like I had slipped off a back pack full of cement I'd been carrying around for a very long time.

There were so many first times for me with you. The first time I sucked cock and really loved it, it was you who had strapped it on for me. I loved it so much that sometimes I would come just from sucking you. It would make me so hot, the way you would talk to me, tell me how good my lips felt wrapped around your shaft, how skilled my mouth was working you up and down, how sexy I looked with tears running down my cheeks, gagging on your cock as you fucked my face.

It got crazy for a while, like I had caught some kind of cock sucking fever that left me with bruised and dirty knees. You had just started packing on a regular basis. You would walk through the door and my eyes would go to your crotch. My mouth would start to water and my knees would just buckle. I had to have your dick in my mouth right there, immediately. I didn't give a fuck if we were in the living room. You would just look down at me, so amused as I frantically unbuttoned your fly, trying to get at you. You'd lean against the nearest wall, grab my hair and guide your cock out of your pants and into my mouth in smooth, slow motion.

How can I explain the strange mix of comfort and lust this produced inside me? The tension in my jaw as I opened to accommodate you, the silky feel of your silicone on my tongue, the panic that was always there the moment your cock head hit the back of my throat, stimulating my stubborn gag reflex. How can I explain how fully I felt your energy, as well as the actual cock, penetrate my mouth, that it was never pantomime, never just imagination? That's why I was crazy about it; the cock was *yours*.

You were the key I'd been waiting for. Other guys had tried to figure me out, but I was a mystery even to myself. I played the submissive girl, but there was always something held back, no one really touched me. I was a master of walls, my internal landscape a labyrinth that I let my lovers wonder through, knowing full well they would never find the heart. You had a height and breadth of perception that was shocking. Smooth like cream, you broke me down and laid me out, held me to your light to see what I was made of.

You were the first person I let fuck my ass, which was something I'd always reserved for my self. My pussy and I never got along so well, ever since the time I tried to pop my own cherry in isolated queer desperation. Later, I could open to lovers, my muscles relaxing with the need for their big hands shoved up inside me. It never worked the same when I was by myself.

It surprised me when I started experimenting with butt sex alone, how intensely I liked it, how I would get off in record speed. My second surprise was when I quickly surpassed my first butt plug and felt how easy it was to shove three, well lubed fingers up my asshole.

But it wasn't something I could do with someone else. Ass fucking seemed so intimate, so potentially embarrassing. And until you, no one had ever challenged that boundary.

You worked me slow and steady, like a glacier on a mountain range, eroding my self-consciousness bit by bit. You had a plan and you were constantly implementing it.

First, you would give my ass attention any way you could. When I was sore from standing up all day at work, you would give me these rub downs that always claimed to be full bodied, but somehow always wound up focusing on my butt. After a beating with your hand or your belt, you would cool me down, kissing, licking, and caressing my welts. "Did you bathe today?" became code for, "Can I lick your asshole?"

You told me you couldn't care less about messy butt sex, you just wanted to fuck my ass. Finally, you bought me a large bulb syringe to clean out with and a 1 1/2" diameter butt plug. You even told me that when we used it together I could take the plug out in private afterwards if I needed to. You were such a gentleman.

But the fist time you fucked my ass with your cock, it was all my idea.

I knew it was something I wanted and I knew I wanted it from you. And even though you had made it clear you would move mountains to get in my ass, I wanted to make it easy for you. I wanted to gift it to you, wrap this particular virginity in a bow and hand it to you on a platter.

So I made the date with you, whispered my intentions into your ear so you would know what was up, so you would come prepared.

When you walked into my room that night I was lying on my bed, naked, on my stomach, reading a book. I heard your boots on the stairs and my skin broke out in goose bumps. You walked into my room and I heard you moan low in your throat, seeing me exposed for you. You crossed the floor to my bed and I automatically fell into a game we sometimes played. I ignored you and tried to look like I was interested in my book. I knew it was the right thing to do when you said, "Keep reading."

I didn't even look at you. I twirled a strand of hair around my finger and kept my eyes on my book. You got onto the bed behind me and I felt your hands on my hips, felt your lips trailing kisses across my lower back, down my ass, dangerously close to my crack. I felt your tongue dart out, lick across the line where ass becomes leg, lick towards my center. You spread me open and I moaned, I couldn't help it.

"Shut up, you're supposed to be reading," you said, and ran your tongue across my asshole.

I took a deep breath and tried not to raise my hips up and back them into your face. Your tongue continued to lap at my asshole, circling it, probing with the very tip. You pushed your tongue into my hole and I held myself still, relaxed. You thrust your tongue in and out of my ass, fucking me. You groaned, pulled out and said, "You're so open, baby," and plunged your tongue back in.

Usually, you addressing me directly signified an end to the game, and I took it like this because I couldn't stand being quiet and still anymore. I started rocking back at you and you wrapped your hands around my hips, pulling me into you. You reached under my body and found my clit hard and slippery and so desperate for your attention. I pulled my knees up under my body and thrust my hips back at you hard, told you how much I needed you, how much I wanted you. You grabbed for the lube, squirted it all over your hand and thrust two thick fingers up my ass. You worked my hole hard and fast, knowing I was ready, that I needed you like that. I leaned back onto your hand, wanting more, fell into your lap and felt your hard-on against the back of my thigh. You held your hand against your crotch, putting pressure on your dick as you let me fuck myself onto your fingers.

Knowing I needed more, needing more yourself, you slapped

my ass and pushed me forward onto the bed. Your fingers slipped out of my hole, making me want to cry. I heard you unzip your fly, I heard the squirt of the lube bottle. I felt the cold of fresh lube on my asshole, and then the pressure of your cock head pushing in.

My muscles relaxed for you and you thrust your cock home, pumping slowly in and out, and then faster as I thrust back at you. You grabbed my hips, holding me still, setting your own pace, running the show. You teased me by slowing down, making me beg for you to fuck me harder. You slapped my ass and told me that you had waited so long to get your cock up into this sweet hole that you were going to pace yourself and enjoy it.

It was all bullshit, you were as worked up as I was, and you didn't make me wait long for the hard, fast fuck we both needed. You didn't make me wait long before you snaked your hand under my body and rubbed my clit until I came, screaming, muscles tense around your cock.

I guess the thing that gets me, makes my heart ache, is how much trust there was in our sex. How much I trusted your love, how respected I felt by you. Maybe I had always thought that loving someone like that would make sex boring, but our sex was the hottest I've ever had.

I still don't really understand how so much love and passion could transform into so much anger and resentment, or how I could have lost track of you over the years. I do know that I never quite shook you loose from my heart, that I still think of you with an aching loss.

Even though I'm always hoping that I'll run into you, I have no idea what I would say. For a while there, so much of our conversations had nothing to do with words. The words were just a structure for all the feelings that we poured out through our eyes at each other every time you met my glance. I wonder if we could still communicate like that. I wonder if I packed this whole letter behind my eyes and radiated it out to you, simply saying, "I've missed you", if you would understand.

Undone

There's this woman I work with. She moves around with more confidence and self-possession than anyone I've ever seen. Sometimes I think it's because she's in her late forties, older than most of the people I hang out with. But who knows? Maybe she's always been that way.

She works in the bulk department at the grocery store I cashier for. I love to find excuses to sneak into the back and watch her, the muscles in her arms tense, as she hefts the 50 lb bags of dry goods around. She has this old school butch feel, and in this town, old school butches might as well be unicorns.

After she got hired, my work clothes got a lot more interesting. My skirts got shorter, my jeans tighter, and this is really saying something. Plunging became the best adjective to describe my necklines. I started wearing more make-up to work, but drew the line at heels after spending most of a shift barefoot when I decided it was more comfortable than standing eight hours in front of a cash register in stilettos.

I would watch her move around the store, her short graying hair tousled and messy, like she'd just rolled out from between some girl's thighs. She drove me crazy. My mind would start running in circles. Did she date femmes? Would she even recognize me as femme? Or would she think I was some young, freaky straight girl trying to fuck with her? She looked like the exact kind of trouble I liked, but outside packaging can be deceiving. What if she wasn't a top? Lord knows she inspired bottom space in me.

I turned on my best flirt.

At first, I don't think she knew what to do with me. Then she started playing along, seeing what I'd do. When I didn't run for the hills, but continued flirting shamelessly with her, she turned up the volume. We'd be alone in the back room and she'd start dirty talking me, nothing too nasty, just enough to make my breath catch and my cheeks burn. The way she looked at me made me want to get down on my knees before her, my wrists held together behind my back, and show her what a good girl I could be.

It was crazy making, wondering if she was going to make a move, ask me out. Maybe she had a wife. Maybe she thought I was too young. Maybe she didn't get hot for curvy girls. Maybe she didn't get hot for femmes. The possibilities for rejection were endless in my head.

Then came the night we were on inventory together and the third person working our shift called in sick. I almost pissed myself when I walked around to the back of the store and saw her sitting on a stack of crates, smoking a cigarette. I always did inventory with the same two people. I hadn't even bothered to check the schedule and I was totally unprepared to see her. She squinted at me through the smoke, looking me over like I was dessert on legs, like she wanted to devour me right there.

I was like a bunny in headlights, my aggressive flirty self dissolving like the ground giving way beneath me. I said hi and fumbled around, finally saying something about getting to work, and walked past her into the building. Habit kicked in and I managed to work my ass a little extra, hoping she was looking. I thanked the sweet Goddess that I was wearing my brand new skinny jeans that hugged each of my curves like a glove.

I made my way to the office desk in the back, getting my clipboard and inventory list together. I heard her boots behind me as she entered the building, slow and measured, echoing through the back room. I listened to her steps get closer and my body started breaking out in goose bumps. She didn't stop until she was right behind me. My hair was pinned up. I could feel her breath on my neck and smell the smoke from her cigarette. My heart was beating hard and I was working to control my breathing. This woman had me undone and she hadn't even touched me yet.

She leaned closer and whispered in my ear. "Well, sweetheart? You've been flirting with me for months. You want to take this to the next level? Or should I back off and we can start working?"

She was being rather gentlemanly about it, not even implying that I was a cock tease. I didn't know what to say and my breathing wouldn't slow down.

I turned my head and looked at her over my shoulder, trying to let all the built up want for her show in my eyes. She smiled at that, took hold of my shoulder, and turned me around to face her. Her hand came up to stroke my jaw, her thumb tracing my lips. My eye's were locked to hers and I kissed her thumb, opened my mouth, sucking it in as far as it would go. Her eyes blazed and she moved her thumb gently in and out of my mouth. She was working me with kid gloves so far, treating me real soft and gentle, but I could feel the power building inside her, making her body tense.

She took her thumb out of my mouth and spread my saliva back and forth over my lips.

"That looks like consent to me, sugar, but I want to hear you say it."

"I want you," I said. It just slipped out. I wasn't feeling very eloquent.

It seemed like enough though, because she smiled and said, "And what should I do with you, baby girl? Hey, by the way, how old are you anyway?"

This caught me off guard. It was hard for me to remember my own name at that moment, but I answered her, dazed, "25?"

She whistled softly and said, "Damn girl, I'm old enough to be your mother. Actually, you're younger than my daughter."

I was thrown off balance. I did not want to be thinking about this woman being my mother; maybe my daddy, but not my mother.

"You have a kid?" I asked, hoping I didn't sound too shocked.

"Yeah, I didn't raise her though. Gave her up for adoption. I was only 14 when I had her." I could sense everything she wasn't saying in the way her body pulled away slightly, the way she wouldn't meet my eye. I turned her face towards me and kissed her softly on her mouth, letting her know that her having a kid older than I was didn't stop me wanting her. She ran her hands over my hips, pulled me into her. I moaned into her mouth, I couldn't help it. I was so turned on I felt shaky. I could feel my pussy dripping puddles into the crotch of my jeans.

She broke the kiss and tilted my head back to get at my neck. She kissed me lightly, leaving a trail of moisture from her parted lips. Then she was at my ear, nuzzling me, whispering, "What do you want, sweetheart? What can I do for you?"

I started blushing furiously. I managed to whisper, "I want you to rough me up."

"Yeah?" she said. I could hear the edge of tension and

excitement in her voice. "What does that mean to you, baby? Give me more."

"Ummmm," is all that would come out of my mouth. My face was still hot and I bit my lip, not meeting her eye. Why did this woman make me so nervous? I looked down and noticed the wide leather belt she was wearing. I felt my pussy clench as the inspiration hit me.

I slowly raised my eyes to hers.

"What is it, girl? You can tell me."

I took a deep breath and blurted out, "I want you to hit me with your belt."

She smiled and leaned back against the wall, crossing her arms over her chest. She said, "Are you going to let me fuck you too, or do you just want me to hurt you?"

I wanted to spread my legs for her right there, show her how wet she was getting me. Instead, I tried to get a hold on myself and said, "No, I definitely want you to fuck me." My voice was still shaky.

"Are you going to be able to tell me if I do something you don't like, or if you want me to stop? You want a special word or something?"

I wanted this so bad and I wasn't in the mood to pretend I didn't. "No, I don't need a safe word," I said. "I'll just tell you if I want you to stop."

"All right. Take off your pants."

My fingers trembled as I undid the fly of my jeans and wiggled them over my hips. I left my panties on, since I hadn't been instructed other wise, and I was sure there was a huge wet spot spreading up the front.

Arms still across her chest, she looked me up and down. "Lean over that desk and stick your ass out for me." I did as she said, pushing the papers and clipboards to the side. "Spread you legs wider." I spread my legs as wide as they could go, my back arched. The air felt cold on the soaked crotch of my panties.

I heard the leather of her boots creak as she pushed off from the wall to stand behind me. "Damn, this is a pretty picture." She hooked her finger under the crotch of my panties and ran her knuckle up and down my slit. We moaned at the same time, hers like a growl, mine a whimper in the back of my throat.

I wanted more, I wanted her whole hand inside me, but she took her finger away. Sliding my panties down over my hips, she whistled again, low under her breath. I imagined what she was seeing, my bare ass up in the air, legs apart, my pussy spread open, exposed.

I could hear her unbuckle her belt, sliding it slowly from the loops. My legs turned to jelly. I was glad I was lying down across this desk because I probably couldn't have stood if I wanted to. She trailed the belt down my lower back, across the crack of my ass, the tip brushing my pussy lips. She brought it between my legs and rubbed it back and forth, getting the leather wet with my juices. She pulled it back and tapped it lightly against my thighs, making a wet sticky sound on impact.

"All right, sweet thing. We're going to start out slow, a round of five and then we check in. You ok with that?"

I would have rather she whaled on me, but the words to explain this escaped me. I nodded my head and said, "Yeah, that sounds good."

She didn't hold out on me though. When the belt came down, it came down hard. The first stroke made my knees buckle. My body shuddered at the pain so sharp it drove me crazy, overwhelming me as it quickly turned to pleasure, making my cunt ache, my clit pulse. She followed the first stroke with the other four, crisscrossing my ass.

"You want more?" She ran her hand over my ass, feeling the heat.

"Yes, please? Yes," I said, moving my ass back and forth.

She started really going for it, harder and faster, making me cry out with each hit. She passed the tenth stroke and went on to the eleventh, starting in on my thighs, barely missing my pussy. My body rocked forward with each hit. I was wondering if I could take more when she reached fifteen and stopped.

Her hand felt cool on my ass, tracing the welts. "You're ass looks beautiful all marked up." I could feel her lean closer, scrutinizing the marks. "Damn, girl, you're already starting to bruise! Are you ready to get fucked yet?" Her hand slid down to my pussy, checking how wet I was getting. I pushed myself back at her, trying to get her fingers inside me, but her hand evaded me.

My endorphins were kicking in and I felt more relaxed and more shaky at the same time, also kind of silly. Little giggles were sneaking in between my moans. I bit my lip trying to stop.

"What are you giggling about?" She slapped my ass with her hand, making me gasp. "Do you want to get fucked or not?"

"Yes! Please…"

"Roll over." She slapped my ass again and I rolled over, trying to arrange my sore cheeks on the cool surface of the desk. She grabbed one of the office chairs, parked it in front of my spread legs and sat in it. She leaned back and looked up at me.

"Take your shirt and your bra off. I want to see your tits."

I pulled my shirt up over my head and unhooked my bra, letting my DD's down slowly onto my belly.

"You are so beautiful," she said. One of her hands was resting between her thighs, her thumb running back and forth over the seam of her crotch. "Play with your tits for me, baby. Give me a show."

I could feel my face heat up again, if I had ever stopped blushing in the first place. This woman could make things I had done before, of my own volition, seem new, and so dirty. I lifted my tits up and pushed them together, grabbing my nipples between my thumb and forefinger, twisting and pulling them. I watched her watching me, getting so hot turning her on like this.

She reached up and stroked my thighs, pulling them further apart, spreading my pussy wider. Leaning back, she said, "Come sit on my lap, sweetheart."

I got up from the desk and straddled her lap. She grabbed my sensitive ass and pulled me down onto her, hard, grinding my pussy into the fly of her jeans.

"Ohh, fuck, fuck, fuck," I said.

"I'm getting there, baby, I'm getting there," she chuckled. She held my tits up to her mouth, pressing them together so she could get both my nipples into her mouth at the same time. I leaned back, bracing myself, holding her knees, and rode her lap for real.

"Don't come yet, girl. I haven't even fucked you yet." She reached to her right and grabbed a box of vinyl gloves we use for cleaning and slipped one on. Sliding her hand down to my pussy, I raised myself up to give her access, letting her slip two of her big fingers up my cunt. She fucked me with hard, fast strokes.

I lost it, if I ever had it around her in the first place. I started moaning, loud, my breathing all over the place, too fast. I was losing my war with hyperventilation and I was getting dizzy. She grabbed the back of my neck, forcing me to look into her eyes. "Slow your breath down, honey. Breathe with me." She started breathing real deep and slow, her hand pumping in and out of my pussy slower, but just as hard.

I was whining, feeling like a brat but not able to stop. I tried to breath deeper, slower, drawing the air down to my pussy. It made me even more dizzy. I leaned forward, resting my head on her shoulder.

"You okay, sweetheart?" Her fingers stopped moving inside me. I felt embarrassed. She kissed my neck and shoulder, stroked my back with her free hand. "You want to try something else?"

"Like what?" I asked, nuzzling my face into her neck. I could smell her skin and my lips parted to taste it.

"Mmm, that feels good," she said, her hand tangled in my hair. "I was thinking about how much I would love to eat this dripping pussy of yours." She curled her fingers gently inside me, making me moan into her neck. "Would you like that? You want to sit on my face, darlin'?"

I was still feeling shy. I made an affirmative noise and she guided me to sit up. I angled my hips so she could pull her fingers out of my cunt, leaving me feeling empty. I got off her lap and leaned against the desk, suddenly aware of how naked I was.

She went over and grabbed her coat, one of those jean jackets with the fake sheep lining. She laid it on the floor, positioning herself on top of it so there was plenty of jacket on either side of her head for my knees to rest on. I smiled at her chivalry.

"Come on down, sugar."

My legs felt shaky like a newborn colt. I managed to straddle her face without hurting her or myself. Her hands grabbed my hips, trying to pull me down to her mouth. I giggled and fell forward, catching myself with my hands, raising my ass in the air.

"Come on, give it to me," she said. I lowered myself down to her mouth and felt her tongue part my lips, licking from my pussy hole up to my swollen clit. She sucked my clit into her mouth and swirled her tongue around it in circles. I started humping her face, making her work my clit harder.

It was then that I realized I had to piss. I panicked, not knowing how to stop the action, not wanting to. She stuck her tongue up my pussy and I bounced up and down on her face.

"Oh, fuck, fuck, fuck." I knew I couldn't hold it much longer. I stopped moving and raised myself up off her mouth. "I have to piss, I'm so sorry. I'll be right back, I promise."

Her hands on my hips tightened. "You're not going anywhere." She tried to pull me back down to her tongue.

"I'm serious, I have to piss! I can't hold it!" I felt close to hysteria.

"Don't."

"What?"

"Don't hold it," she said, craning her neck up to get at me, licking my pussy lips. Her tongue went between my clit and my hole, putting pressure on my urethra.

"You want me to piss on your face?"

"Uh-huh."

I was looking down at her, trying to make eye contact. When she looked up at me her eyes were hard, laced with steel. I'd seen that look before during pervy sex. It said, "I dare you to say no, call me a freak, walk out on me."

I wasn't going to say no. I also wasn't going to think about what we would do afterwards, piss covering my legs, her face, her hair, her jacket, the floor. I rested more of my weight on her face and she went back to working my clit, sucking me into her mouth, grazing me with her teeth.

It was crazy, this building of pressure in my bladder and cunt. I let her build me up more. I wanted to come as I pissed, something I had wanted since before I knew what orgasms were, a little girl touching herself while peeing in the woods.

She was lapping at my pussy now, rocking me into her face with her hands, wanting me to let go. Her hands strayed to my ass crack, spreading me open, brushing my asshole with her fingertips.

That was it. I started coming. My piss squirted out of me in spurts, timed with the contractions of my orgasm. I tried to raise myself up, give her the choice not to get it all in her mouth, but she held me down, lapping it up, licking my clit, drawing my orgasm out. It felt like I pissed forever. She kept her face there the whole time, loving every second, rubbing herself into me.

When I was finally done, I rolled off of her and groaned, finding my legs even weaker than before. "I don't think I can walk after that," I said, lying down beside her, curling my naked body around her fully clothed one.

She laughed and held me tight. "That's ok, baby. You can take the inventory on the bottom shelves and I'll take the top ones."

Like We're Making Babies or Some Shit

Row is big, the biggest guy I've ever fucked. She towers above the majority of people, surpassing them in height as well as width. She takes up a lot of space; she can't help it. This has been true for most of her life, and you can tell by the way she holds her body, the confidence she exudes, that somewhere along the way she became used to it.

Her biceps are solid and beefy. I can barely wrap my two hands around them. When we are lying in bed I like to bury my face in her armpit and kiss along the sensitive underside of her arm, trace her tattoos with my tongue. Her back is a paradox, a broad sheet of rock hard muscles covered with soft padding. I've tried to give her back rubs with my tiny hands, but find the territory too daunting, my elbows and knees way more suited for the work.

There is something specific and physiological that happens to me when we are in close proximity. She walks by and my heart beats hard at my blood, driving it to the surface. I swear, I can feel every particle of air displaced by her motion sliding over my skin, it's so sensitive. She wraps her massive arms around me and I go limp, swooning like some wacked-out lady on the cover of a paperback romance novel. And when she rolls on top of me, my legs spread wide to accommodate her, it grounds me like nothing else. Being a big girl myself, she makes me feel small in a way no one has.

See, when I met Row I wasn't used to fucking people bigger than I was. For me, this took our power dynamic out of the theoretical. It took it from a place I went to in my head, giving myself up to someone's psychological domination, and turned it to a real live thing rolling around in the bed with us. In the heat of the fuck, with her holding me down, I can struggle all I want. The only way up is to ask. That's okay though, mostly I don't want up.

Row has big appetites. She eats more meat than anyone I've ever been with, devouring whole animals in one meal, it seems. I can tell it's good for her, it's what her body needs. Even me being a vegetarian, it somehow makes me wet watching her rip apart a steak. She eats her meat rare, still bloody. She likes to ignore me while she's eating and I just sit there watching her, crossing and uncrossing my legs, squeezing my thighs together. She'll look over at me every now and then, licking the juice from her fingers, and say, "You hungry or what, baby?" Like it's the meat I want, when she knows damn well it's her I want to sink my teeth into.

It's not like she ever keeps me waiting long. Like I said, the guy has big appetites. She likes to fuck, all the time, day or night, public or private. That's okay, though. I like to fuck too.

Really, you can't take us anywhere. Try as our friends might, it just doesn't work out. Take us out for dinner or drinks, 10 minutes into it she has her hand up my skirt and I'll wind up in the bathroom bent over the sink getting my ass fucked. Or, if I'm lucky, she'll be up against the wall with her pants shoved down, her fist in my hair, maneuvering my tongue all over her hard clit. We can't help it. We're both sluts, but together we're always horny.

Trying to drive anywhere is the worst. One time we even drove her truck into a ditch. We were going to her mom's house for dinner, 30-minute drive, but 15 minutes into it she had me frantic. I had my panties off and everything.

It went something like this:

We're going to her mom's house, okay? So, I'm getting ready, trying to look presentable. I like her mom a lot, she's a great lady, not uptight or anything, I just want to look nice. I put on a high wasted skirt, a little below the knee, black, paired with a silk button up blouse, a deep wine color. I top it off with a black cashmere cardigan, soft as a kitten's belly, that I scored at Goodwill. I button the top three buttons, but it's pointless. No matter what I'm wearing, Row always makes me feel like a total slut.

She picks me up in her piece of shit truck, you know the kind, held together with ductape and prayers with mileage pushing three hundred thousand. I grew up with cars like that, the ones my dad or brothers were always working on, trying to get them to pass inspection, trying to get just a little more out of them before they got retired to the back lot for parts. Even though I don't work on them much myself, I've soaked up a lot of knowledge just being around, and I have a few tricks of my own. Like, you'd be surprised how many miles you can go with a pair of pantyhose replacing a shredded fan belt.

Anyway, she picks me up. First off, she pushes her glasses up her nose and gives me a long slow look up and down. There's lechery in her eyes, in the crook of her mouth as she shifts into reverse and says, "Nice outfit." Like I said, she makes me feel like a slut.

Next she starts talking, she knows she can always get me this way. It doesn't even matter what she's saying, it's how she says it. She could be saying anything in that smooth, deep voice of hers and my pussy starts weeping.

This time though, it's not just any old thing coming out of her lecherous mouth. She's telling me how every time she sees me in lipstick she can't help but think about having to scrub it off her cock after our dates, how she'd love to see those lips wrapped around her cock right now. We're going to her mom's, she's not packing, but does it matter? She just wants to see me worked up. I could hold out on her but I don't. She's getting to me and she knows it. I start crossing and uncrossing my legs, squeezing my thighs together.

She tells me how good it feels to come down my throat. "You give really good head, you know that?" she says. "And, fuck, you're such a slut for it. You LOVE sucking my cock. You'd go for that shit anytime, wouldn't you? You can't get enough." It's true; I'm a slut for her cock.

I'm sitting as far away from her as possible, looking out the window. I can't look at her or it will be all over. This doesn't faze her. She can see me shifting in my seat, she can tell she's got me wet.

"You know, if there's one thing I love more than my cock down your throat, it would have to be my cock buried in that tight, wet pussy of yours." She's looking straight ahead, drumming on the steering wheel, nonchalant. "It really gets me when you're all laid out for me, naked, your legs spread wide, and you pull me down on top of you and I slip my cock right up into your pussy. I can look right into your eyes as I rock my dick in and out of you, just the way you like it. That look in your eyes is so sweet, so fuckin' precious. It's like we're making love, like we're making babies, or some shit."

This is a new tactic, and it throws me. I break my rule and look at her. She looks at me, kind of awkward, and that's how I know she is serious. Not like she doesn't genuinely love to fuck my pussy, but this is something different

We look at each other for a second and then she's back on track, "That's when you wrap your legs around me, when you beg me to start fucking you harder, really fucking your pussy. You're so wet I can hear my cock slamming in and out of you. That's my favorite sound, that and your voice telling me to fuck you harder."

I decide it's all over. Like I said, I'm a slut, and Row really brings it out in me. I lift my hips and pull my skirt up around my waist. I slip my lace panties down and off my left leg, letting them dangle from my right as I prop it on the dash. I know I'm going to leave a nice puddle on her seat to add to the years of grime already accumulated there. I slip my finger between my swollen lips. Jesus, how wet I get surprises even me sometimes. I'm not looking at Row. Despite that sweet moment, I'm still pissed that she decided to pull this on the way to her mom's.

But she's looking at me. I can see her out of the corner of my eye. She pushes up her glasses, takes quick peeks at what I'm doing to myself. She licks her lips, unconsciously, runs her hand across the short hairs covering the back of her skull.

My clit is hard and slippery, I can't get enough friction going, but I keep stroking. I want to make this look as good as possible. I arch my back, stick out my tits. I unbutton my blouse, showing off some cleavage. I throw my head back and start moaning while I stroke myself faster, making sticky noises I doubt she can hear over the muffler.

My eyes are closed but I can feel her gaze like it's a tangible thing. Then I feel her fingers brushing my thigh. She has to stretch a little to reach me.

"Get over here," she says, her voice sounding strained.

"No," I say, continuing to rub my pussy, rocking myself into my fingers.

"I said get the fuck over here," she says, her need making her voice, making everything about her hard. "Little girl, get your ass over here right now, or I'm going to beat the skin off of it the next possible moment I get!"

There are two things about this that we both know. One is that she is the only one who can call me little girl. Two is that I love it when she beats my ass.

So, it's not because of her threat that I unbuckle my seat belt and scoot my naked butt over to her. She takes one hand off the wheel and wraps a thick arm around me. I've got my left leg scrunched against her side and my right thrown over her lap and hanging between the seat and the door. I start sucking on her neck, whimpering in her ear as I hump my pussy against her thigh. Her hand kneads my ass and then slips down my crack and underneath.

Her fingers slip into me and I gasp as she starts to fuck me in this crazy position. My hand slides around her gut, squeezing her flesh, then goes to her crotch rubbing her through her jeans. She groans and pushes down on the gas, jerking us forward. She is trying her best to look forward and drive straight. Suddenly she grabs my hand and puts it on the wheel. "You steer," she says, as she buries her face into my cleavage, taking a chunk of flesh between her teeth.

"You are fucking crazy!" I scream. Truth be told, I don't know how to drive so well. Steering is only one small part of driving, you might say, and doesn't seem like it would be so hard, but maybe you've never tried it with fingers up your pussy and a large piece of your tit between someone's teeth.

It all happened so fast. I swerved, she slammed on the breaks and we were in a ditch. It was actually a lot better than it could have been. There was no one else on the road, no cops behind us, no tree for us to crash into. The ditch wasn't deep and we didn't flip over. We were both kind of shook up though. We just sat there for a minute, panting, not looking at each other. Then Row growled deep in her throat and pushed me back onto the seat. Her fingers found my pussy again and thrust home. She threw my leg over her shoulder and fucked me hard and fast, just the way I like it, looking into my eyes, like we were making babies or some shit.

Things changed between Row and me after that. I don't know if it was the brush with death or this new concept of "making love", but we felt more attached to each other, more like a couple. Not that we were any less fuck machines, but we were on a different level with each other, more intimate.

We would kiss a little longer before going for pussy, have real make out sessions, something we'd never really done before. And she got into this thing where she wanted to suck my pussy for hours, all the time. She would spread my legs and my pussy lips and just look at my cunt like she'd never even seen pussy before and it was the most glorious thing on earth. She'd stare at me so long I'd get impatient with feeling her breath on my clit and I'd start wiggling my hips, begging her to lick me. Then she would, with a long, soft stroke of her tongue, starting at the base of my hole ending at my clit. After that, she'd go for it. She'd wallow in that shit for hours if I let her.

Before, sucking my pussy, though obviously enjoyed by her, was about making me cum. Now it had shifted, it was more about her need for my pussy in her mouth. Not that I'm complaining, it's just that sometimes she would build me up to excruciating heights and not let me come.

I'm the kind of girl who needs some things to get off, you know? I need your tongue to lick me just the right way, at this pressure, your fingers fucking me at thing angle, this spot. I just know what I like, okay? And so does Row, the guy had me down by day three, she had me coming like I'd never stop. So, this shit was deliberate.

I mean, it's not like I mind being teased now and then, I love it. It just got a bit much. But then I developed this strategy, and it's worked out pretty good.

It looks something like this:

She's had me on my back for a while. Her face is between my thighs, her lips are wrapped around my clit, sucking on it with the slightest suction, her tongue circling the head with the lightest touch. I'm moaning and rocking my hips into her face, thrusting my clit into her mouth, but she's still working me with a touch I can barely feel.

So I say, "Baby? My back hurts, and I bet yours does too, being in that position so long. Lay back and let me ride your face for a while. Please, baby?"

At first I thought this would give me more control over how she licked and sucked me, that's how it's always been in the past. If I want it hard, I can grind my pussy into the face I'm riding, if I want it lighter, I can back up. Not with Row, though. She gets her big hands right in there and holds me open and right where she wants me, about 1" away from her mouth. She continues her tease, licking my pussy lips, licking my hole, licking a careful circle around my clit. I put up with this for a while, thrashing and moaning above her, and then go to stage two.

"Baby? If I turn around, will you give my ass some attention too? Please, baby?"

Now, the guy loves ass almost as much as pussy. I shift position, straddle her face with my big ass in the air and stretch out along her body. I spread myself wide for her, giving her good access. She spreads my cheeks wider and runs her tongue lightly over my puckered hole, licking at the center, pushing the tip into me. This makes me wild, makes me crazy. I'm laid out over her body and I'm backing myself into her tongue, clawing my nails down her legs and moaning my head off.

The best part of this position, and my ultimate goal, is I have access to *her*.

Now, Row has some kind of old-fashioned ideas. I say 'old-fashioned' because, it's not that she doesn't like having her cunt touched once in awhile, it's that she thinks she shouldn't like it. She was raised by some old school butches who had pretty strict ideas about gender and fucking. It's a something she's been chipping away at for awhile.

I love being on my back for her, giving up my body for our mutual pleasure. There are plenty of ways I can get her off without flipping her, some of them without even touching her. But there comes a time when all I want, all I can think about, is her cunt in my mouth, her clit, swollen and hard between my lips. Our dynamic doesn't even have to shift. In fact, the times hottest to me are when she grabs me and uses my mouth for her pleasure, just grinds into me, fucks herself into my mouth and comes into me. I love sucking her cunt; I'm more of a slut for it than I am for her cock.

So anyway, I'm laid out on top of her, ass in the air, straddling her face, feeling her tongue on my asshole, and then back on my pussy. She has access to both, so she takes advantage, alternating between ass and cunt. My eyes are focused on where her legs meet her body. She's in her boxer shorts and I can see a wet spot, her juices soaking the crotch. She shifts her hips and the fly gapes open a little, exposing her dark pubic hair. I can smell her and my need gets big and swollen, making me gush in her mouth. I lower my face to her crotch and just nuzzle her a bit, testing her mood.

Immediately, she starts working me harder, her tongue now on my clit, licking a little faster. She spreads her legs slightly and angles her hips up at me.

This is my invitation and I go for it. Spreading the fly of her boxers I take her big clit in my mouth and suck it, work it with my tongue, moan into her. Her taste sends shivers down my body and makes my hips twitch involuntarily. I want her juice all over me, want to suck her down my throat and swallow.

Any way you look at it my motivations are selfish. I want this guy in my mouth, want her pulsing clit under my tongue, want her taste, her smell, her juice rubbed into my skin, her come in my mouth. Also, I want her so excited that she licks me to orgasm; I want us to come simultaneously in each other's mouths. Typical fantasy, but there it is. Sometimes you got to go back to the basics.

So, finally, we're really going at it. She's got her hands on my hips and she's pulling me into her mouth, sucking my pussy, lapping my clit at a steady pace. I'm holding her lips open with my fingers and sucking on her clit in short, fast bursts, nursing on it, just the way she likes it. Her hips are thrashing into my face, she's going to come soon.

And suddenly it's too much. I'm so hot, so turned on by her

open and wet under my face, so built up from her teasing my cunt for an hour, that I swear, it wouldn't matter what she was doing, it wouldn't matter if she stopped, I would come anyway. I would come just from her taste, from her smell, from the silky feeling of her wet under my tongue. And I do. My hips drop down and I grind my clit into her mouth, blood pulsing hard through my body. My tongue is still between her lips and I cry my orgasm into her cunt.

While I'm coming my technique gets sloppy, but now I feel how close she is and I go for it, licking, sucking like I could do this all night. She's humping her clit into my mouth, and I suck her in, holding her firm, as her abdomen starts trembling. Her hands are locked around my skull, holding me to her. Her come is starting and I can feel it peak and come crashing down, making her holler and shake. Her hands are so big I wonder if she could crush my skull if she squeezed just a little bit harder. Row comes hard.

After she relaxes her grip on my head, relaxes everything, flops boneless on the bed, I give her one last kiss and feel her clit jump under my lips. She swats at my ass feebly, weak and dazed from her orgasm. "Get up here."

I dismount, swing my leg up and over, turn around and wrap my arms around her. We kiss long and slow, our cunt juices combining in our mouths.

"Goddamn," she says, licking her come off my lips, my chin, giving me a spit bath. I giggle, roll onto my back and pull her on top of me. I hold her close, wrap my legs around her, and let her weight pin me solid to the earth.

Shopping

I woke up that hot summer morning with my toes inside Cole's mouth.

My brain was slow to catch up. We had a date planed for that morning, but she hadn't slept over the night before and I wasn't expecting to wake up to her sitting on my bed. Her soft tongue played between my toes, pulling me out of the sticky slumber my brain was lost in. My body started responding before the rest of me became conscious. My hips were already moving in small circles and my legs were trembling. I opened my eyes, moaning as the nerves in my toes relayed the sensations straight to my pussy. She slid her tongue over my burgundy lacquered nails, slipping my first three toes in and out of her hot, wet mouth.

"Morning, princess," she said when she saw my eyes open, nipping her way down my instep with her teeth. I smiled and stretched sleepily, arching my back. I could feel my thighs slip against each other from more than sweat as I shifted my position.

"You naked under that sheet?" Her hand slid down my leg and I parted my thighs for her. She lifted the sheet and peaked underneath as her thumb played over my sticky thigh, just shy of my pussy. I spread wider for her, hoping she had come over to fuck me.

"Damn, beautiful, you got wet so fast." She ran her thumb over my slit and brought it up to her lips, sucking it clean.

"You know you drive me crazy sucking my toes like that."

She grinned at me, but made no move to touch my cunt again. Instead, she slapped my thigh and said, "Get up and put on something pretty. I'm taking you shopping."

"What?!"

"Girl, you heard me, don't make me repeat myself."

I was so confused. I had never been shopping with her, let alone been taken shopping *by* her. I never liked the idea of dates buying me things. I'd seen too many relationships where "gifts" of money and material objects played out in twisted and manipulative ways. I had watched my mother play that game with boyfriend after boyfriend. I wanted no part of it. I thought I had talked to Cole about this, but it hadn't really come up much. Between her own bills and her mom's, who she helped support, she was always broke.

I sat up, letting the sheet fall away from my body, and made my way to where she was sitting at the end of the bed. "Are you trying to tell me," I said, straddling her lap, "that you came over here, woke me up, got my pussy sopping wet, and now you want me to get dressed and leave my house without even getting fucked? What kind of shopping?"

Her arms, strong and dark from working so much in the sun, circled around me, pulling me close to her. I noticed she was packing a very large cock under her jeans. What the fuck was she planning?

She reached up and touched one of my hoops, hanging from my ear. "Baby, how the hell do you sleep in these things? They are huge!"

"You're changing the subject. Answer my question."

"Which one, you asked at least two." She pushed my messy locks and earring out of the way and started kissing on my neck. It felt crazy good, especially when she started sucking the salt off my skin. If she really wasn't going to fuck me, I wasn't interested in being more turned on than I already was. I grabbed her hair and pulled her off me.

"Answer me!"

"Okay! Okay! Yes, I want you to get dressed and come out with me. I'm going to fuck you, but not yet. I just got paid and I want to take you shopping. Since I'm running this date, I can take you wherever the fuck I want and don't have to tell you shit. Now do you want to cooperate and play nice? Or are you going to be a total pain in my ass all day?" She leaned back a little, smiling, waiting for my answer.

"I'll show you a pain in the ass." I lunged forward, trying to push her flat to the bed and get her twisted over so I could spank her. She was too quick, too strong, and too ready for my bullshit. She wrestled me down to the bed and I shrieked with laughter as she pinned my arms down to my sides.

"Bitch, you are incorrigible," she said, laying her body on top of mine.

I smiled up at her and spread my legs, letting her weight fall directly on my naked pussy. I got in a few good grinds against her denim-covered bulge before she raised her hips out of my reach.

"You are such a slut," she laughed, kissing my nose, "and I love you. Now get up and get dressed for me."

She let me go and I huffed up off the bed. She usually took every opportunity to fuck me senseless and I couldn't understand why she was being so resistant to my charms. I was also nervous about what this shopping would entail, and how the very obvious bulge in her jeans fit into the picture. I decided to play along, for now.

I was tempted to draw out the process of choosing my outfit, but decided to get it over with, picking a halter-top that barely contained my tits and a short denim skirt. I brushed my hair and went to the bathroom to piss.

I was just finishing applying some eyeliner when she opened the door. I turned to face her, eyebrow raised, a nonverbal question. She closed the distance between us, one hand on the back of my head pulling me into a kiss, the other up my skirt, caressing the parts of my ass that peaked out from under my panties. Her tongue slid into my mouth, soft and slow. My knees went wobbly and I felt pussy juice soak my panties.

She pulled back, a smile in her eyes, turning up one corner of her mouth. "You look beautiful, let's go."

Our first stop was this hip shoe store downtown. We walked in and she made a beeline to a display of heels, heels I'd been lusting after for months. They weren't just any heels, but a new design from this orthopedic company that were supposedly easier on your body. Sexy, stylish heels that wouldn't fuck up my already fucked up joints? Maybe it was bullshit, but I was willing to fall for it. These shoes were expensive though, like 15 times more than I was used to paying at the Salvation Army. I hadn't even been able to justify starting the process of saving for them yet; something else always seemed more important.

I hadn't told Cole about my tortured love affair with these shoes and I racked my brain trying to remember who I had told, and how she knew to hold up the exact style I wanted and ask the sales woman for a pair in my size. I didn't even know she *knew* my shoe size.

When the woman ducked into the back I said, "Baby, these shoes are too expensive, I can't let you buy these for me."

Her eyes got stern on me. "I'm not going to argue with you."

The woman came back with the box and handed it to me, then returned to the front of the store to help some people who had just walked in. Cole sat down in a chair and crossed her arms over her chest, determination setting her face. "At least try them on for me."

I looked at her and bit my lip. My lust for these shoes was winning out. I slipped off the shoes I was wearing and opened the box. God, they were beautiful, black leather, opened toed, thin ankle strap. The heel was substantial and not that high, maybe 2 1/2", but the thought of being able to wear them for hours in relative comfort, walk around in them, was dreamy. Most of my time in heels was spent on my knees or flat on my back

I bent down and slipped one on, buckling it around my ankle. It was perfect, the leather so soft it left me breathless, my heart beating fast. "Here," she said, "let me do the other one."

I handed her the box and placed my foot in her lap, balancing on the one shoe. I glanced over my shoulder. The sales woman and the other customers were absorbed in their shoe selection. I turned back and moved my foot directly over her cock, running my toes up and down her shaft, pressing down with my arch, pushing the base into her clit. She let out a little grunt and quickly got the shoe out of the box and onto my foot, buckling it smoothly.

My stomach dropped, like I was on a roller coaster. Putting my feet into these shoes was like putting my hand up someone's cunt. It was like fucking.

"Walk around for me, sugar."

I walked around the store, swinging my hips, trying to feel out the chances of rolling my weak ankles. They felt pretty solid. I wanted these shoes, but I still felt weird about her buying them for me. I decided to try to talk some sense into her one more time.

I sat down next to her and got as far as, "Baby..."

She sighed in exasperation, grabbed my chin and kissed me softly, once, on my lips. "Listen to me." Her hand on my chin, her eyes serious. I couldn't look away. "I love that I don't need to buy you shit to keep you happy, I love that you are resourceful and that you made half the clothes in your wardrobe from scratch, but baby, YOU CAN'T MAKE THESE SHOES." I started to laugh, I couldn't help it. She smiled her crooked grin. "I respect you as an artist, but you just don't have the skills to make shoes like this. Besides, you're always saying that butches should learn how to support femmes. I'm just supporting your gender expression, sugar... and if I'm supporting my own sexual fantasies at the same time, well, we both win don't we?"

Buying us shoes wouldn't be on the top of my list of ways I think femmes need to be supported, try acknowledgment and respect, but I was done arguing. "Fine, baby. Fine."

I sensed the sales woman hovering and turned toward her as she said, "Are you all set?"

"Yeah, we'll take them," Cole said. "You want to wear them out, honey?"

"Yes." There was no way I was taking these babies off.

She paid and we were out in the heat again, my new heels clicking on the sidewalk.

"How do they feel?"

"Like sex."

"That good, huh?" She laughed. "I'm glad you like them."

I stopped and turned to face her. "Baby, I don't even know how to thank you." Suddenly I felt like I was going to cry.

"Hey," she pulled me over to a bench and sat me down. "Honey, sugar, darlin', it's nothing, its just money! It's a gift, not some fucked up thing I'm going to hang over your head until I squeeze some gratification out of you. It's not like that. I'm not trying to be your sugar daddy, I just wanted to buy you some pretty shoes. Okay?" I nodded my head. It made me feel better that she was starting to understand my discomfort, even if I was having a hard time articulating it. "Now I want to buy you a new bra and some panties, so lets go to the mall."

"The MALL?!" I was really being a pain in the ass today, but the mall makes me crazy, really, it gives me panic attacks.

"Come on, girl! I promise we won't be there long, and I'll get you a snack if your blood sugar drops."

We were walking into the mall when I balked, thinking of another potential disaster.

"Cole, you do realize that a lot of the shops in here don't even carry clothes in my size, right?" My body inhabits that chubby region where if "regular" stores sell clothes that fit me, they're usually the largest size they carry.

"Relax, sugar, I have taken big girls shopping before, I'm not completely ignorant to the injustices of mainstream lady's fashion."

Well, that about covered it.

She pulled me into a shop, an "intimate apparel boutique" the sign said. It wasn't Vicky's or Fredrick's; I had never been in there before. The woman behind the counter looked us up and down in clear disapproval and said, tartly, "Let me know if I can help you."

Was it our sweaty, tattooed bodies? Our blatant

homosexuality? My slutty attire? The bulge in Cole's pants? Who knows, but she was definitely not into us.

Cole steered me over to a rack of bras in the corner. I wondered if she had scoped this store out in advance. She started flipping through the bras. "What's your size, honey? 40, 42? D, DD?"

"I don't know. It depends on the brand."

She held up a burgundy bra with a black lace panel down the middle of the cup. I thought my tits would fit in there, but it would be a tight squeeze. "I want you to try this one on." She turned to the cranky lady at the counter. "Can she try this on?"

"That's what the dressing room is for," she said in singsong condescension.

"Jesus," Cole said under her breath.

She pushed aside the curtain, but before she could go in, the woman up front shouted, "Only one person in the dressing room at a time!"

We looked at each other, our eyes narrowing, contemplating what we should do. Finally, Cole said, "Well, sugar, you're just going to have to come out here and show me."

I smiled, knowing we were about to cause a scene, feeling ready for it.

By some miracle, the bra fit. Well, my tits definitely bulged out the top a little, but it basically fit. The lace panels were not completely see-through, but the outlines of my hardening nipples were definitely visible. I pushed the curtain aside and stepped out of the dressing room.

Dripping my words in sugar and projecting loud enough to reach the front of the store, I said, "What do you think, baby? Do you like it?"

I ran my hands over the sides of my breasts and under, lifting them slightly.

Cole rubbed her chin in mock consideration. "Hmmmm. Turn around for me, sweetheart." I spun around in a circle, catching a glimpse of the clerk, her face red and her eyes glaring fiercely at us.

"I don't know. Is it too tight around the bottom?" She reached over and ran her fingers under the elastic, her thumbs brushing over my nipples in an obvious manner. I heard the clerk gasp. "No, I think it fits good. We'll take it."

I stepped back into the booth, unhooked the bra, and tossed it out to her before closing the curtain. I heard her chuckle and her boots clunk to the front of the store as I put my halter back on.

When I came out the clerk was still beet red and her lips were pursed tight. As she shoved the bra into the bag, she spit out, "If it were up to me, I wouldn't even accept money from you people."

"You have a lovely day as well," I said as we walked out, my hand sliding into the back pocket of Cole's jeans. Confrontations like this always leave me feeling giddy.

Getting panties was less eventful, and much more within my comfort zone: a cheap three-pack of cotton thongs from Target. I was a little surprised when she picked them out. I didn't even wear thongs, though I had been mighty curious ever since a friend of mine described the experience as feeling "like you're getting rimmed 24/7". We passed a bathroom and she handed me the bag.

"I want you to put on a pair of these panties and meet me around the corner, third store on the right."

"Will I find a hidden envelope with my name on it containing further instructions?" I was still feeling silly.

Cole rolled her eyes. "Just do it."

I found a stall and took one of the thongs out of the package. My panties had been up my ass all day anyway; the thong didn't feel too different. I wouldn't exactly say it felt like someone licking my asshole. The narrow crotch did feel nice against my pussy, and I wondered what the hell Cole was planning and how long it was going to be before she fucked me.

I left the bathroom and rounded the corner, stopping in my tracks when I saw what was third on the right. It was a knife shop. My heart started pounding in my chest and my breath went all fast and shallow. I stood in front of the shop looking in at the blades, trying not to drool or whimper out loud. Cole was at the counter, her back to me. I managed to stay steady on my feet as I crossed to her, putting my arm around her shoulder. There were three knives in front of her on the counter.

She turned to me, nuzzling my neck, and whispered into my ear, "I want a knife to use on you, just for us. I want you to pick which one you like."

I wondered if my knees would give way right there, if I was blushing, and if people would know how turned on I was or if they would think I had sunstroke.

All three knives were beautiful, but the middle one drew my eye like steel to a magnet. It had a beautiful pearly handle, swirling blues and grays. The blade was slender and curved up slightly at the tip. I could see myself reflected in the shiny steel as I leaned closer.

I pointed to it. "That one."

We got out of there as fast as we could without running. She led me down a street, down another, pushed me into an alley, behind a dumpster. We were both breathing hard as she shoved me up against the brick wall.

"You still want to get fucked?" She had her body pressed up against mine, her thigh parting my legs and rocking into my cunt. She sucked on my neck, biting me, and I let myself moan and lean into her. I felt frantic. I dug my nails into her arm, clawed at her back. She was sucking on my neck like she was going to leave it purple and swollen and I wanted her inside me NOW.

"Please, baby? Please fuck me? I need you inside my pussy so bad."

She stopped chewing on my neck and leaned back from me, keeping me pinned against the wall with her hand on my shoulder. With her other hand she flipped the knife open and brought the blade to my throat.

The bottom half of my body felt liquid and I whimpered, not because I was scared, but because my need for this blade was so big I saw red. For that second I wanted to push against that sharp edge until it sunk into my neck like butter.

"Don't worry, slut, I'm gonna fuck you." She ran the knife lightly across my neck. I could feel the blade slicing through cells on the very surface of my skin. She backed off me completely, leaning against the dumpster, the knife dangling casually from her hand, and looked me up and down.

"Sit down on those crates." There was a stack two high next to me and I sat down, leaning back against the wall and spreading my legs slightly. "You're going to have to spread farther than that if you want me to get at you."

She knelt down in front of me and pushed my skirt up above my hips, allowing me to spread my thighs to their furthest extent. Slowly, gently, she slipped the knife blade underneath the crotch of my new thong, angling so the dull side was pressed against my pussy. I gasped as she ran the edge up and down my slit. The sharp point scraped against my thigh where it came out the other side of my panties, making me shiver. She hooked her finger underneath the crotch and pulled it away from my body as she sawed through the cotton with the sharp edge of the knife.

"Mmmmm, your pussy is so beautiful." She turned the knife upside down and slid the handle between my pussy lips, sliding it up and down, the bottom of the handle bumping my clit.

I couldn't take it any more. "Please, please, please, Cole, please!"

She slipped the handle into my hole, fucking it in and out of my pussy. It didn't feel like much, but it drove me crazy seeing the blade sticking out of my cunt, her hand holding it carefully. I wanted her to fuck me hard with it, but she kept sliding it in and out at a controlled pace. I felt desperate by the time she lowered her mouth to my clit and sucked it gently into her mouth with the slightest pressure. Despite this tease, I came hard and fast, thrusting my hips into her face.

She put the knife away, hauled me up, and slammed me back against the wall.

"You ready for something bigger up your pussy?"

She unzipped and took her dick out, pulling my leg up over her hip and pushing her cock roughly up my pussy. I was so wet and open and ready, her roughness was exactly what I needed.

84

She fucked me hard and fast. I started talking dirty in her ear, wanting her as worked up as possible.

"Yeah, fuck me, baby, fuck me. Don't stop. God, you feel good. Your cock is so fucking hard. You feel so big filling up my pussy. You feel how wet I am for you?"

"Yeah, I feel how wet you are. Jesus, fuck, your pussy feels good, so tight and hot and wet wrapped around my cock. You like getting fucked hard, don't you, slut. Don't you?"

"Oh yes, baby, yes. Fuck me, don't stop, baby, don't stop. *Please.*"

"Oh, I'm not going to stop. I'll fuck you all day in this alley, if I have to. Fuck, baby, I'll fuck you all night. I'll fuck your pussy so raw you won't be able to walk for days. As long as I have to, girl. I'm going to fuck you until you come for me. Come on, baby, give it to me. Give yourself up for me."

She started pounding into me harder. The base of her dick was rubbing against my clit, quickly bringing me to the edge. I could feel how turned on she was and I wanted to bring her over with me. "Baby, I want to feel you come inside me. Oh, fuck, yes, please, baby, please, you're gonna make me come, fuck, fuck, fuck."

She quickened her strokes and pushed me over. I was coming hard when she started moaning and bent down, biting the top of my tit where it pushed up over the top of my halter. That sent me spinning into a new set of spasms. I cradled her head to my breast, stroking her hair as she finished coming inside me.

I held my breath as she pulled her cock out of me. I would be sore for days, and I could feel where the brick had rubbed the skin off my back. I wiggled out of the remains of the thong and threw it into the dumpster. My legs were shaky on my new heels as we walked out from the alley, hand in hand, but I was ridiculously happy.

August Crazies

My Ac had fallen out the window the week before and the air was thick and heavy. I didn't want to move, but was filled with this August restlessness, worse than any spring fever I'd ever experienced.

It had me wanting to claw out of my own skin. It had me collapsed on my bed holding a bandana full of melting ice to my forehead, wishing Bren was getting home tonight and would come over and fuck the shit out of me. It had me regretting living in a town too small for dyke bars where I could go and feel anonymous. Instead, I was stuck with coffee house lesbo folk nights where all my friends and most of my lovers past, present, and possibly future would be congregating tonight.

I had been debating whether to go or not for an hour and it was suddenly too much.

"How fucking boring!" I said this out loud and propelled myself off the bed with a force that would have surprised someone if they had been watching me a second before. My indecision was getting on my nerves as much as the heat. I grabbed a towel and headed for the bathroom, sweaty and naked, my thighs sticking together with each step.

I slammed the door to the bathroom, not that there was anyone home to hear it. Teresa was at work and Em was as out of town as Bren was. "Fucking Bren," I muttered, turning the shower on and adjusting it a little warmer than cold. What's the use of having a lover if they aren't there to fuck you senseless when the August heat is making you crazy? I stepped into the shower and gasped as the water hit my chest and ran down my body. My nipples turned to hard little pits and I squeezed them roughly, thinking about Bren's biggest cock and how I wished she was here to fuck my face with it till I choked. Damn, tomorrow was too far away.

I could see if Hawk was free for a date later, but as good as it would feel to beat the shit out of her right now, what I really needed was someone to beat *me*. Hawk would hit me if I asked her to, but it was different from getting beaten by a top. There would be none of the hardcore domination that I craved with my bruises. "Fucking Bren!"

I washed quickly and got out of the shower. I had about an hour before people would be showing up at the café, plenty of time to get decked out. If I couldn't get the fucking I needed, at least I could make everyone there wish they were coming home with me. I started laughing at that thought and almost tripped on the stairs up to my room. I had known everyone in this town for years, and if there was an attraction, it had been negotiated already.

Maybe a date with Hawk wouldn't be such a bad idea, I mused, going through my closet. But I knew better. Hawk was an excellent lay, but was too submissive to give me what I needed tonight. All her cocky little boy attitude flew out the window the minute I started topping her. The guy wanted to be bossed around. This was hot, but felt like work tonight. Mostly our dates were about me hurting and fucking her, and going there would give me the worst case of blue balls. Fuck anyone who says femmes can't get blue balls.

To my surprise, the music had already started and almost everyone was there by the time I reached the café. Hawk and Teresa were outside smoking when I walked up, and I could hear the acoustic guitar through the walls.

"Damn, roommate," Teresa said, spotting me first. "You look fine."

She was looking pretty fine herself, clad in a short skirt and tube top exposing the beautifully inked tattoos of red Bee Balm covering her chest and shoulders.

"Hey, love," I said as she rose and gave me a kiss. "How was work?"

"Boring and stupid, per usual." She stubbed out her cigarette and smiled to let me know she was just bitching, that her day hadn't been that bad. She gave me a hug, maneuvering herself towards the door. "I gotta piss, baby. I'll see you inside."

Hawk was still smoking and she gazed at me with barely concealed lust. She looked like she had come straight from work at her uncle's. She worked in his garage on the weekends, doing oil changes and learning mechanics, and her pants were covered with petroleum and grime. I wanted to climb onto her filthy jean covered lap and hump her till I was coming out my ears. Instead, I sat down next to her and kissed her cheek as I ran my fingers through her short, sweat damp curls.

"How are you, sweetheart?" I could see a definite blush creeping across her cheeks. Too fucking cute, I wanted to drag her into the bushes and kick her ass right there.

She looked at me shyly from under her lashes. "I'm fine... how are you?" She took my hand and brought it to her mouth, kissing my fingers with soft, dry lips. It was all I could do not to go for her throat.

"I'm crazy, baby. I'm going totally insane. The heat is making me tired and cranky and horny. I don't feel comfortable in my own skin. I feel lethargic, but totally manic at the same time." I felt a small tremor go through her at the word 'horny'.

"Is there anything I can do for you?" She looked at me with hopeful eyes.

"No, baby." I took her face between my hands and kissed her softly on the lips. "Just be sweet to me tonight. I can't take this mood out on you, it would end bad. You're so fucking tempting though." I grabbed the short hairs at the base of her skull, tugged gently, and then let her go.

She relaxed and reached for her tobacco. Reading my mood like the excellent bottom she was, she asked, "When's Bren getting home?"

"I don't know, sometime tomorrow I think." I felt distracted, and like I needed to get away from her before I changed my mind and dragged her into a corner to fuck.

Rolling her next smoke, she said, "Maybe you should go inside and get a beer, try to relax."

I kissed her cheek again, wiped off the trace of lipstick I'd left, and got up to go inside. The woman on the low stage was playing a haunting song and crooning about lost love. I decided to give in to the downer part of my mood and sat next to Teresa, set on brooding and soaking up the music. I briefly fantasized that some handsome butch from out of town would be playing tonight and need a place to stay, but everyone was from the area, no surprises. Besides, sleeping with someone who didn't know me when I was in this mood would be a horrible idea.

Teresa got up to get some tea and I looked around the room to see who was here. I saw Teresa get in line and start grinning and waving to someone behind me. I craned my neck to see who she was waving at and the bottom fell out of my stomach.

"Bren! What the fuck are you doing here?"

She chuckled softly and shook her head. "Such language out of such a pretty mouth. Come back here and say hi to me."

I rose and stumbled to her seat, trying to decide whether I cared about making a scene by throwing myself on her lap. I settled for sitting down as close to her body as I could get. She wrapped her arms around me and I buried my face in her neck.

"Did you miss me, angel?" Her words came out husky with tenderness, and suddenly I wanted to break down and sob.

She leaned in close to kiss my lips, but some bratty, angst-ridden part of me said, "Don't fuck up my lipstick."

She gave me a look of exasperation and rolled her eyes. "Baby, I'm your butch. If I fuck up your lipstick, it will be intentional." Then she leaned in and kissed me so sweetly it felt like my connective tissue would dissolve and all my bones clatter to the floor.

Leaning back, she licked her lips, erasing any sign of my lipstick, regarded me and said, "Perfect."

"Darling, do you really want to stay for the rest of the show?" I ran my hand along her collarbone, just under her shirt. I wanted to be next to her bare skin so badly.

"Uh-uh, you?" She was smiling like she had followed all my frustration that day.

"No." I shook my head emphatically.

"We could go to the bar and get a drink." Her knowing smile was infuriating. She was fucking with me and I wasn't in the mood.

I leaned close to her ear and dug my nails into the back of her neck. "I want you to bring me home, beat my ass, fuck me, then suck my pussy till I come in your mouth." Call me bossy, but I had to show her my need was serious.

In one smooth movement she stood up, reached for my hand and asked, "Shall we?" I let myself be guided out the door.

I caught a glimpse of Hawk on my way out. She was standing with her primary lover, an older butch named Toni, and she flashed me a knowing smile seeing me leave on Bren's arm. It's funny having bottom solidarity with someone you top. It can be mindboggling, the complexities of identity, desire, and where they intersect in poly relationships. It can make you pull your hair out in frustration, make your heart break from all kinds of nasty feelings as we try to rewrite the horrible stories we were raised with. But when it works, when the puzzle clicks together, when everyone involved feels respected and taken care of, it can create a kind of triumph that leaves you high for years.

I blew a kiss to Hawk on our way out.

Bren was all nonchalant warmth on the walk home, telling me about her trip, asking me what I'd been up to. I would have been fooled except I *knew* her, and I could feel the tension coiled in her muscles, emanating off her body. Damn, she was smooth though.

We walked in the door and she asked, innocently, "Is Em home?"

"No, Em's still-" I said, right before she grabbed me and slammed me hard against the wall. I felt all my my breath leave my lungs in a squeak.

"Good, then she won't have to hear you scream." Her voice was warm and smooth, but her eyes were hard and I could see the muscles in her jaw twitch. Her fingers were digging into my upper arm so hard they would leave bruises. I whimpered, overcome with the intensity between us, overcome by how fucking scary she got in this mood.

Her body pressed me into the wall and she grabbed my throat, squeezing hard. "You greedy little bitch. Five minutes home and already you're bitching at me to fuck you, suck you, beat you. You're such a selfish little slut."

She looked at me out of hard eyes, breathing deep. A cruel smile twisted her mouth and she slowly ran her thumb over my lips, smearing my lipstick across my face. I felt blood rush to my cheeks.

"Get up to your room." Any warmth was gone from her words and she grabbed me roughly and threw me towards the stairway. I stumbled in my heels and she viciously pushed me forward. The heat hit me like a wave at the top of the stairs, making it hard to breath. She marched me over to my platform bed, which was the perfect height to bend me over.

I was shaking and whimpering by the time she pulled up my dress and ripped my panties down to the middle of my thighs. I couldn't see her, but I could hear her trying to control her breath. Then I felt her hand on my ass and my shakes became violent. She reached between my legs and grabbed the crotch of my underwear, pulling it towards her until the lace cut into my thighs.

"What's the matter baby, are you cold?" Her other hand trailed down my shaking back. She leaned down to my ear, twisting the panties in her fist, and said between clenched teeth, "Or are you just scared I'm going to give you what you asked for?" She pushed up off the bed. I could hear her unbuckling her belt, sliding it from the loops. In the midst of the August heat, my teeth began to chatter.

"Tell me your safe word," she demanded.

"Uncle," I stammered. So far our age play had not included uncle/niece dynamics, and 'uncle' had always been my safe word wrestling with my brothers growing up. It was easy to remember, ingrained.

"Do you want to use it?" she asked.

I shook my head emphatically and felt her hand grip my hair, wrenching my head up and twisting it until our eyes met.

"I said: do you want to use it." Her voice was like chips of flint and she punctuated each word with a vicious shake of my head.

Through trembling jaws I said, "No, Sir." She was definitely Sir tonight; there were none of my daddy's tenderness in her words or actions.

My answer was evidently accepted, because with a final shake that left me dizzy, she released my head and brought the belt down with a loud crack. No warm up, no foreplay, she brought the leather down hard. I jumped with each hit, the pain too much, too fast, making me tense up, which only made it hurt more. I tried to relax into it, but despite my talk, I wasn't all that used to full-on beatings with no preliminary. I tried to count her strokes in my head, but couldn't concentrate. I tried to breathe through the pain, but felt like I was hyperventilating. I tried to ground, tried to send my energy down, and in the center of the craziness found calm reassurance that I was getting exactly what I needed.

"Fuck, I love beating your ass. I love how fast you welt up, how fast you start bruising. I love how your ass jiggles and shakes every time the belt hits you." Her words were colored with passion and the exertion of the beating. She was gradually moving from the top of my ass down, her strokes overlapping. When she got to the juncture between my ass and my thighs the vibrations of each hit made my pussy burn. That's when I realized I was wet, so wet, dripping down my thighs. My endorphins must have been kicking in because the pain was starting to feel good, different from the good of pain just for pain's sake that I had been craving that day. I started relaxing and rocking into the hits, my whimpers transforming to moans.

"That's it, cunt. Rock that hot ass back for me." She brought the belt down harder than she'd ever hit me, three times, one on top of the other, where the curve of my ass turns to leg. It ripped me out of my pleasure haze and sobs welled up in my throat. It took me a second to realize she had stopped hitting me and I jumped when I felt her fingertips tracing my welts.

"Oh, sweet love. I'm so lucky to have a girl like you," she crooned. Who was she now? Was this my daddy talking? Her fingers traced down my crack and dipped between my legs to find me wet, overflowing. "Oh, fuck, baby. You liked that, didn't you?"

Her fingers plunged into my cunt and she pumped them in and out, fast and hard. My pussy was making hungry slurping noises around her fingers and she added another one. I was open and sucking her into me. She fucked me harder and murmured encouragement to me as I fucked back at her and tried to take her hand.

"I missed this pussy so much when I was gone," she murmured. "Did you miss my fist, baby?"

I was moaning and fucking myself onto her four fingers. It occurred to me that she needed this as much as I did, that she had her own frustrations built up in her body that could only be released in violence, that had to be taken out on my ass and in my pussy.

"Tell me how bad you want my fist," she said, her fingers pumping into me. "Tell me how much you want my hand inside your pussy."

I felt like I could never be full enough. I felt like I wanted both her fists inside me buried up to her forearm. All I could say was, "Fuck me, fuck me, fuck me."

Abruptly, Bren pulled her fingers from my cunt and a sob burst from my throat. She slapped her hand down on my ass where the skin would be black and blue tomorrow. I realized my mistake, and through wracking sobs I tried to rectify it. "Please Sir, please fuck me?"

"Too little, too late. Come on, you can do better than that."

"Please, Sir," I didn't know if my words were intelligible through my tears, all I knew was that I needed her fist inside me and I'd babble anything to get it. "Please, Sir, I want your fist inside me so bad. Please baby, please Bren? You know how much I love your hand inside me, you know you make me come so hard. I love you, baby, I love the way you fuck me. I need to come with you inside me. Please make me come, please Daddy? I need your fist so bad, I need my daddy's fist inside me." I broke off, sobbing so hard I couldn't talk. I barely knew what I was saying, who I was saying it to. Maybe I thought if I appealed to the multiplicity of who my lover was to me I would make my need known. There was something horrible and divine about being made to beg for what I wanted. My heart swelled along with my clit at the mix of shame and the total surrender to love that it produced inside my body.

"Tell me how much you need it."

I was shaking, choking on my tears, "I think I'll die if you don't fuck me, I need you so bad."

She laughed, standing there behind me, and some small animal part of me froze, recognizing a meanness in her that startled me.

"Poor little slut, I doubt it's that bad." She ran her fingers over my welts, hard enough to make me shy away from her. "You'll have to prove it. You want me to fuck you, you'll have to work for it. Convince me."

Her hand was on the back of my neck, her fingers twining in my hair. Time felt strange, slowed down, then sped up as she wrenched my head back and pulled me off the bed. I had one of those weird out of body perspectives, seeing myself shaking and crying, make-up smeared all over my face, staring wild eyed up at her from my sudden position on the floor. The vantage point made her look taller.

She looked down at me, in a heap at her feet, disheveled, snot running down my face, and sighed. "We can't have this," she said as she roughly squeezed my nose, wiping the mucus from my face and tossing it on the floor.

I started bawling harder and she looked at me with disgust. "Look at you crying in a heap on the floor." She nudged me with her boot. "I know I train my sluts better than that."

I was broken down into warring factions. There were parts that wanted to cry myself into oblivion, parts that wanted to beg for the privilege of licking her boots for hours and a sudden rebellion that was all for leaping up and decking her. Submission has always been a mixed bag for me.

I chose the path of least resistance and arranged myself with my sore ass perched on my heels and my wrists together behind my arched back. I kept my eyes downcast, not only to complete the submissive picture, but also to hide the spark of defiance I knew was clearly visible.

"Much better," she said, stepping forward until my forehead rested on the rough denim of her crotch. The pulse quickened between my thighs and I moaned being so close to her. Something in me softened and I quit fighting myself, gave up any notion of fighting her.

Her fingers tangled themselves into my hair and she pulled my head back. "Are you ready to prove it, baby? Prove how much you want my fist?" Her voice was low and sweet, a disorienting contrast to the pain building in my scalp. "I'll make it easy on you. Just nod your head."

It wasn't easy, of course. She was holding my hair so close to the scalp that the motion was barely possible, but I did the best I could.

"Good girl," she purred, and with her free hand, pulled down her zipper. I moaned and tried to lower my head to see what she was uncovering, but she held my head firm, forcing eye contact. "Listen, bitch, here's the deal. You are going to suck me off like you want me to fuck your pussy. Satisfy me and I'll take care of you. Understood?"

She released her hold on my hair and I nodded, feeling the tears drying on my face. "Yes, please," I said, feeling calm for the first time in days.

She smiled down at me and pushed her jeans and briefs off her hips. "Pull these down for me, will you?"

I was quick to oblige and groaned as the smell of her hit me. Her hands cupped my head and I got a quick view of her glistening thighs and swollen clit as she guided my mouth onto her.

It was all pretense, all a game. She knew I would lick her to orgasm any time, anywhere. It was something I begged for, drooled for, a service I would perform at the slightest hint she wanted me. The mind fuck was for her more than me. The psychological domination broken into the right code words to navigate the traps in her head and make it safe for her to drop her pants. But I would be lying if I said it didn't make me hot as fuck, if I denied the aching pulse in my clit as she pulled my face into her cunt and rocked herself back and forth between my lips, running the show. Nothing is ever simple, never only what it is on the face of the thing. Our insides were spread wide inside a room of mirrors, reflecting ourselves back to each other over and over, a writhing mass of pink and red organs.

I moaned into her cunt, vibrating sound off her clit. She was breathing heavy above me, groaning deep in her throat as she pulled my face into her. I lapped at the shaft of her clit, avoiding the sensitive head, circled around it, then sucked it into my mouth and licked her with fast strokes, using the very point of my tongue.

Her hands tightened on my head and her hips stilled, holding me exactly where she wanted me. I felt the tension building in her abdomen, felt her muscles quiver and begin to shake. A moan starting deep in the pit of her stomach escaped her mouth as her hips jerked forward against my mouth. I increased the pressure of my lips around her clit, pressed her hard with the flat of my tongue, felt her gush down my chin as she came in my mouth. Her body lurched forward, and she bent over as the contractions rolled through her.

As she relaxed I kissed her, nuzzled her pubic hair, ran my hands over her shaky thighs. She straightened her body and took a deep breath, gently pulled my face away from her cunt and looked down at me. "I love you so fucking much," she said, and I knew she was Bren now, just Bren, and I was just me, her girl.

She pulled me up and led me over to the bed, stripping me of my clothing as we went. Gently, she pushed me back onto the mattress. The sheets felt surprisingly cool against the heat of my newly beaten skin. I spread my legs wide for her, showing her how wet I was for her. The time for begging had passed, but I looked up at my love's face and said, "Please, baby? I want you to fuck me so bad."

She crawled up on the bed with me. I tugged at her shirt and gave her a pleading look. She chuckled and pulled the shirt over her head, tossing it on the floor. I ran my hands over her bound chest and tugged at the fastenings, unwrapped her like the only present I had ever wanted. She kissed my lips softly, slipping her tongue into my mouth, her hand trailing my jaw, pulling me towards her. Her hand went between my spread thighs and her fingers pressed at my opening.

My blood pressure spiked and I groaned through gritted teeth, "Yes, please baby. Please fuck me, please."

She grinned down at me and thrust three fingers inside my pussy, pumping me hard, no longer making me wait. She felt so fucking good, and I told her so. I thrust my hips, raised them up off the bed to meet her hand and she added another finger. I felt full, and like I would never be full, never have enough of her inside me.

Her mouth was right above mine, breathing my breath, breathing my moans and whimpers, running her tongue along my lips. "More, baby, please more, I want all of you," I said into her mouth.

I felt the muscles at the mouth of my cunt burn as she added her thumb and pushed her knuckles against my opening. Maybe my pussy was bigger in my mind. Maybe the juice gushing from my cunt was too watery for such intense penetration. Maybe I didn't give a fuck about any of the obstacles, I was going to take that big fucking hand of hers up into my pussy if I tore myself doing it.

She rotated her hand, twisting, rubbing her knuckles all around my opening. I felt like I was about to black out, or fly away, or forget my own name.

On cue like she read my mind, Bren started chanting my name, told me to give it to her. She coaxed, calling me *sweetheart-sugardarling*. She demanded, calling me *bitchslutwhore*. She said my name and my cunt opened up and she slid her fist inside me.

She rocked her fist, rotated her hand, making me twitch and moan. I clenched my muscles around her wrist, drawing her in. She groaned deep in her throat and pumped her fist against the resistance of my tightened opening. My world narrowed to a sensation of pressure so deep and wide, pleasure and pain held in an open palm, related but separate enough to be different. My cunt was full of bittersweet and with one right move I would explode.

Bren made it. She rocked her fist upward, her knuckles kneading into the spongy tissue on the roof of my pussy, and it set me off like a firecracker. Shock waves spread out from my cunt making me shake and spasm. Her rocking fist kept me anchored, grounding me in the intense sensations of my body. She fucked me through my come until it got too much and I squeezed her hard with my muscles and begged her to stop.

I opened my eyes, not knowing I had closed them. It was dark in my room and I was drenched in sweat, drenched in come, dizzy and high from the fuck. An early night breeze was coming through the open window, sweet relief, swirling through the thick heat of the air. Bren's skin was sticking to mine everywhere that we touched and she was quiet beside me, her hand playing with my hair.

"I missed you, angel," she said, and kissed my sweaty cheek.

Second Date

It is our second date and I still don't know what to call you as your fingers wrap themselves around my throat. You haven't told me and it didn't occur to me to ask. My back is pressed firmly against the wall of this hallway and as your hand squeezes, your lifeline heavy on my windpipe, words well up in my mouth like saliva. *Yes, please, more, thank you,* and behind them this desire to name you, name exactly what you are to me in this moment.

Sir feels most safe, standard, but there is a little girl deep inside me who has already claimed you for her Daddy and that word feels large and weighted in my mouth, a stone held protectively underneath my tongue. This girl is desperate to know what she has done to make her Daddy so angry he would wrap his fingers around her throat, constrict air and blood, choking out his sweet-princess-baby-girl-sugar-darling in the hallway between kitchen and living room. Because this is what she wants to be to you: treasured and precious and small and cared for, Daddy's angel, sheltered in his strong arms. Made to do unspeakable things, knowing she is safe because her Daddy would never truly hurt her... not really.

The problem is, I haven't told you about her yet. The problem is, while you are my perfect wet-dream butch Daddy, I have no idea if this is a role that has found a place within your desire.

I have told you about other aspects of my need to submit. The part of me that is loving every ounce of brutality dealt by your hand, that longs for force and velocity to bring your palm to my cheek, that wants your teeth sinking deep into the meat where the base of my neck joins my shoulder. Tomorrow morning I want to wake up to a visible map blooming on the surface of my skin, undeniable evidence of where we have been.

I've told you that I like to be roughed up during sex, told you what kind of pain I like and to what degree. I have not told you about how this kind of treatment has the tendency to open this deep and vulnerable rawness inside me, cracks me open like a pomegranate, my red jewels spilling everywhere.

Because, baby, it has been awhile since I let a butch touch me like this and it is only our second date, and I like you way too much for the small amount of time I have known you. I am not ready to be cracked open for you, all seeds and red juice, all that potential sweet and tart and available. I want to stay inside my own skin, contained, private. I do not want to be that girl who gives you access to her pussy and her heart on the same night.

But your hand is so many things grabbing my throat. It is sweet and delicious and causing this fierce panic to blossom in my stomach. My heart is swelling and cracking open and I know that all of this is visible in my eyes. I can tell that you have recognized what you are seeing when your grip relaxes to a caress and you ask me, *You all right honey?*

This and the tenderness in your eyes could undo me, could reduce me to a sobbing mass on the floor. But I am committed to this course of action, determined to have sex with you tonight without breaking open, without making accessible the tender regions beneath my ribs, and without the word *Daddy* accidently slipping past my lips.

So, *Yeah, fine*, I say, pushing past you and heading for the bedroom, pulling my dress over my head, hoping to distract you with skin and curves and flesh spilling from foundation garments.

While I haven't known you long enough to fully realize exactly who I am dealing with, I get the feeling as you cross the room toward me, your eyes intently locked on mine and no where else, that I should have known better than this. That I have highly underestimated you if I think I can get away with smoke and mirrors, this slight of hand like my internal process is a shiny coin I can hide up my sleeve. I am not wearing sleeves and your hand is hot and dry where it grips my bare arm, your other hand coming to rest on my cheek as you continue to look me in the eye, gaze sharp, mouth quirked slightly at the corner.

What's going on in there, darlin'?

I see calm and confident strength in your eyes, a soothing counter balance to this anxiety riding the swell of feeling inside me. That look in your eyes makes me want to believe in a world where I was never labeled 'too much', where that fertile and messy and powerful landscape of emotion is not only tolerated, but maybe accepted and a little sought after. I want to believe in a reality where you can handle me, in all of my parts. My insides ripe and accessible, burst open and artfully arranged for you on a platter.

I make a decision and say, *Can we just talk a bit?*

Your head nods and I take your hand and lead you to the couch. I tell you a story of a little girl whose needs were not met, of a teenager bleeding internally. How she was told that she cried too easily, cared too deeply, laughed too loud, and wanted too much. I tell you how that little girl inside me wants so badly to feel cherished and cared for and as the words *want* and *Daddy* come out of my mouth, you pull me deep onto your lap and cuddle me close.

This one gesture is like salve on old, festering wounds. Layers of neglect, calcified like limestone, start to loosen and prepare to slough off.   I lean my head against your chest and breathe in your cologne as you stroke my hair, musky sandalwood, a suggestion of pepper.   I let myself relax and feel what this safety is like, even though I know it is a fleeting thing.   I am a grown-ass woman, struggling to integrate my past with my present, and wanting desperately to embrace my future. This small moment of time, relaxing into your lap, being held in your strong arms, is a precious gift.

My nose is pressed against your neck right above your collar and I shift so my lips fall to your skin.   There is a low rumble that comes from your chest, a purr or a growl, and your hand tightens on my hair, tugging at the roots.   My tongue snakes out to taste your skin and you groan, *Sweet baby, you wouldn't tease your Daddy, would you?*

My body turns into yours, my tits pressing against your chest on my mouth's way to your ear.   *No, Daddy.   I just want to make you feel good.*

I rock my ass into your lap, feeling what you packed for me. Your hand grips my jaw and you kiss me for the second time ever.

Your tongue slips inside my mouth and this small entrance into my body triggers a massive need to have as much of you inside of me as possible.   It feels like summers when I was a kid and would cram as much Bubblicious bubblegum inside my mouth as would fit.   I would work my jaw furiously, chewing the wad, and loving the feeling of my mouth so full.   At the same time there was this inexplicable and overwhelming desire to swallow the whole mass down my throat and this is what your tongue in my mouth is like.   I want to swallow your tongue to make room for your fingers, your cock, your cunt, hard and wet underneath, whatever part of you I am allowed to bring into myself.   I want to bring you into myself, want to be stretched by you, filled to capacity, brimming over.

In this moment of feeling overwhelmed I whimper around your tongue and you stop, say, *You all right, Princess? Does it hurt?*

Yes, Daddy. I feel small and fragile and hovering on the verge of panic. I am walking an edge here and while it looks like your desires are the mirror image of mine, I am still terrified I could lose it all.

Show me where it hurts, baby.

I hide my face in your neck and mumble, *It hurts everywhere, Daddy.*

Show me.

I sit up and point to the spot between my breasts where the pain is radiating from, right over my beating heart. Your lips are so soft when you lower them to my skin, your hands firm on either side of my ribcage. My heart is beating so fast under your lips and I can't seem to get enough air into my lungs.

I gasp out, *Daddy, that's making it worse!*

Your eyes are saturated with desire and your voice is a rasping husk. *Where else does it hurt, sugar? Tell me where I need to make it better.*

There is a conflict of need inside me. My little girl is turning my cheeks bright red, ashamed of how much she wants her Daddy's hands in forbidden places. The masochist inside me wants you to slap me across the face as hard as you can, hold me down over your lap and spank my ass until I bruise, then fuck my pussy with vicious precision. Anything to drive me deep inside my body and quiet this overwhelming internal cacophony.

I start to hyperventilate and you sandwich my face between

your two hands. You give me a shake that is both small and fierce and say, *None of that, now. Use your words, baby girl.*

You take a deep and obvious breath to show me the way and I follow your example. When I have some breath back, I lean in and whisper, my cheek flaming hot against yours, *It hurts between my legs.*

You clear the tension from your throat. *That sounds serious, darlin'. I better take a look.*

You lay me down, my back sinking into couch cushions. You peel my panties away from my body and when you spread my legs my hips feel spring loaded, like a bear trap. Your brow creases in mock concern as you stare down at my pussy, holding my legs firmly open so they won't snap shut.

Hmmm. It is really swollen down there, sweet girl. Does it hurt more here, your thumb strokes my clit, *or here?* Now the circumference of my opening.

I am squirming out of my skin. I am shy and breathless and desperate and I want you everywhere at once. *It hurts both places.*

That is serious. But don't worry; Daddy's going to take good care of you.

The tears well up in my eyes all on their own and they are spilling down my cheeks before I can stop them. You lie down on top of me, your hips spreading my legs wide, and trace the tear's path down my face with your thumb. I try to hide my face from you but there is nowhere to go. You grab my chin and make me look at you. *None of that,* you say, *I want to see it. It's sexy when my little girl is so open and vulnerable for me.* You rock into me, a small, slow movement. It is just enough to feel the hardness of your cock through your jeans and suddenly I am on fire.

Oh Daddy, please. The tears continue to stream from my eyes as your hands swallow my wrists and bring them up over my head.

Please, what, baby?

You continue your slow motion rocking and I am trying to thrust myself against you, but your weight is solid pressing me into this couch, hampering my movement.

Please Daddy, please, please…

The dam has burst and my mouth is on autopilot and it feels so fucking good.

Tell me what you want. I want to hear you say it.

I feel little and grown at the same time.

I want you inside me, please Daddy? I want your cock inside me.

The noise that comes out of your mouth is both amused and satisfied. You lower your lips to mine and your tongue is in my mouth again, thick and hot and then gone.

I'm not sure you deserve it yet, you say and suddenly your weight is being removed from my body. Before I get the chance to feel completely unmoored, your hands are there, pulling me up to sitting and back onto your lap.

Suddenly I am all petulance. *I thought you said you would be good to me*, more tears welling up in my eyes, hot and embarrassed.

I am full-on pouting and you chuckle and bounce me on your lap. *I am being good to you, sugar. I'm giving you exactly what you need.*

There is a bubble expanding in my chest and I give into it, letting it pop and come out as a sob. You make mock soothing noises, still laughing at me, but it feels somehow safe and incredibly sexy that you are being mean to me like this.

You let me cry it out, your hands roaming over my body, and as my tears slow to sniffles, you ask, *You want to prove yourself, baby? You want to show me how much you deserve your Daddy's cock inside you?*

All my petulance is cried out and I cannot think of one thing I would not do to please you and show you that I am deserving of your attention.

I lean in and nuzzle your neck. *Yes, please, anything.*

You sigh, *Sweet baby, you almost make me want to go easy on you.* Your hand fists the hair at the back of my neck and you force me down and over your lap. I am all adrenaline, heart expanding, blood pulsing between my legs, angling my ass up underneath your palm.

If you want to be my sweet little princess, you better take this spanking for me. Your hand that is not on my ass is firm on the back of my neck, pushing my face into the couch, and you squeeze down for emphasis. *Show me how brave you can be.*

Yes, Daddy. My ass is moving against your palm in anticipation, and then empty air as you raise your hand and let it fall with a loud smack on my bare skin. You repeat this again and again, the pain hot and sweet, sharp and then diffuse in the moments I am allowed to process it. I am counting in my head and then losing track as you begin to concentrate on my sweet spot and every slap of your hand sends vibrations deep into my cunt. I have never been so close to coming from a spanking before and when you stop so abruptly I cry out in protest.

You maneuver past my legs and out from under me. You are behind me and your cock is out of your pants, the head pressing against the opening of my pussy and then filling me up. Your hands are pressing me face first into the couch, holding my wrists together at the small of my back. I am already on the verge of coming, and although I don't know you yet, don't know your body and the signs that would herald your approaching orgasm, I am guessing by the way you are frantically thrusting inside me that you are close too.

I am about to ask you permission to come when you growl out, *Come for me baby, come on, give it to me*, and I am undone. I am tumbling over. I am screaming and spurting and messy and burst open and I am whole.

The Suitor

There was nowhere in the world Marriander would rather be than the training yard. Her feet could not take her there fast enough, nor her hands work swiftly enough to rid her body of the ridiculous formal silks her handmaiden Amelia had forced her to dress in earlier that morning. Tears of frustration streaked her face, and the sky, heavy with immanent storm, mimicked her internal tumult. She could see Hildegard entering the weapons house just south of the yard, where she now headed.

Marriander burst into the store house, her hair swirling in the quickening winds, eyes wild, a small storm all her own.

"Reception went well, did it?" Hildegard asked with an infuriating lift of her brows. The older woman was tall and broad shouldered, with a weathered, amicable face. She wore her hair cropped close to her skull, a style favored by warriors. Despite her notoriety as one of the queen's most skilled champions, people routinely mistook her for a man.

Marriander snarled at her, an impressive act for the princess, considering the old warrior was twice her size and had killed scores of people in the Queen's service. But, Hildegard had as much as raised her since she was nine years old, and the princess felt more comfort in her presence than anywhere else.

She was in nothing but her undergarments by this point and Hilde threw her a pair of leathers. She ripped the pins from her hair and furiously gathered her long tresses into a braid that she proceeded to knot securely at the base of her neck.

"It was horrible, as I knew it would be! Pompous fools!" She struggled into the leather trousers, ripping her corset and fine linen shift from her body and flinging them from her. "I will never forget the feeling of their slimy lips on my hand. The saliva didn't even have time to dry in between their noxious kisses."

Hildegard barely managed to transform her bark of laughter into a cough before saying, "Now Marri, you are a princess, you've known for years that this day would come."

Marriander whirled on her, "Not you as well! Please, spare me, I get enough of that hogwash from Mother, I don't need it from you."

Having secured the last of the straps on her vest she went to the sword rack and reached for her favorite blade.

"None of that now. We fight with wood today. You will not be touching steel in the mood you are in." She hurled a wooden blade, end over end, and Marriander snatched the hilt from the air.

"But I haven't had to use a practice blade in years!" she wailed.

"You haven't been in this kind of a snit in years," the warrior said calmly. Her seamed and scarred face was full of compassion, and while Marri appreciated her sympathy it did little to bank the fire raging inside her.

She stormed into the yard just as the first fat drops of rain began to fall.

"At least the rain is likely to keep your suitors away, pampered lot that they are. I was expecting droves of them after the reception," Hildegard said behind her.

Marri snorted, "Only one in ten has ever lifted a sword, judging by the softness of their hands. I wonder if they employ that ghastly buttermilk soaking regiment Amelia was always trying to force on me when I was younger."

This time Hilde's barking laughter exited her mouth unimpeded. "If only five of our kingdoms princelings are acquainted with swordsmanship, we are living in dire times. Surely you are being dramatic, my Princess."

"Oh, am I?" Marri lunged, putting the full force of her rage behind the blow. Hilde dodged it easily, sending her full tilt into the rail surrounding the practice yard.

"Have I taught you nothing, Marri? If you must fight when you are angry, channel it. Do *not* let it gain ascendance." She landed a smart blow to Marri's gut, pulled at the last second, but knocking the wind from her nonetheless.

Marri knew she would be covered in bruises by evening and she relished the thought. Nothing would please her more than to surrender to the physical pain of a good fight and forget the panic rising inside her. She let her anger, her fear, and her rising despair sink into the background and allowed her training and her instincts take over.

They circled each other, exchanging blows, relaxing into the familiar dance. Marri delighted in the fluid grace of her body and the stretch of muscle, each blow she managed to land on Hilde's person an affirmation of her skill. Sometimes, though she'd never admit it, she let Hilde slip past her defenses, craving the flash of pain, trusting Hilde to never injure her grievously.

When the rain became driving, Marri backed off, panting and rubbing rainwater from her eyes. She noticed a figure standing in the western corner of the yard, leaning against the rail watching them. Hilde followed her gaze and called a greeting to the stranger, who pushed off from their perch and walked over.

Marri saw that it was one of the lordlings. She had met the fifty lord's sons sent to woo her affections just that morning, but the tedium had rendered individual detail unmemorable. She had a moment's anxiety trying to place this one.

Staring into the stranger's rich, brown eyes, she concluded that he must be one of the exaggerated five princelings who were trained fighters. He wore plain riding leathers, suitable for the training yard and she tried to remember him from the crowded reception hall and recall what he had been wearing earlier that day. A vague impression of the young man dressed in red so dark it was almost black came back to her.

"Who are you?" she asked bluntly.

"Torin of Surrain, at your service," he said, undaunted by her rudeness. His hand was hardly larger than hers, but equally calloused and surprisingly warm despite the air's chill and the fact that he was soaked through. "Care to spar?"

They faced off.

The lordling fought well, if in a style strange to Marri. Midway through the bout something began to take shape in Marriander's mind. Something in the way Torin moved that felt familiar and yet incongruous. It finally struck her that his center of gravity reminded her of Hilde's, as opposed to the lads that she sparred with.

"You're a woman!" Marriander exclaimed.

Torin grimaced and pressed her. "No," she said, thrusting past her guard and forcing her to jump back a pace. "I'm not. Or, not like you mean anyway," she added, stepping back and wiping the rain out of her eyes.

"You're like Hilde," Marri asserted.

Torin glanced over her shoulder to where the warrior stood watching them, sheltered in the doorway of the shed. "Yes. More like Hildegard."

Marriander lunged forward, knowing she was being dishonorable, but needing some small victory today, however won. She landed on top of Torin in the mud, her practice blade at the lordling's throat. Both were panting, blinking the rain from their eyes. Torin's gaze was calm but intent staring up at Marri, and then she broke into a grin that affected only the left side of her mouth.

"My, Princess, do you topple all of your suitors into the mud like this?"

"Are you truly my suitor, then? Or are you here for more nefarious purposes?" The thought had only just occurred to her.

Torin's face turned grave. "I am here as your suitor, truly."

Marriander sat up, her legs straddling the lord, knees resting in the mud. "But what of heirs? Surely the queen is going about all of this madness for the sole purpose to see me bloated and pregnant with the kingdom's future!"

"There are precedents," Torin said, referring, Marri assumed, to the handful of love matches between those of the same sex, scattered throughout the kingdom's history like currents in a pastry.

"But they were all in love! You can make no such claims, we've just met!"

"This doesn't stop you from taking advantage of me, throwing me to the ground and molesting me in the mud," Torin said, bucking her hips, sending Marri inches into the air and reminding the princess the exact region on which she was perched. Hastily, she swung her leg off of Torin and sat next to her. She scanned the yard to see what Hildegard was making of all this, but the old warrior was nowhere in sight.

Marri leapt to her feet. "The Queen will be having a fit about now, wondering why I'm not soaking in a bath of perfume in preparation for the ball this evening."

Out of courtesy she reached out to help Torin to her feet. The lord's hand was still shockingly warm.

"I must go," Marriander said quickly, turned heel and fled.

That evening's wardrobe was even ghastlier than the one for the morning's reception, though slightly easier to move in as she was expected to dance all evening. They still made her wear a corset; lightly laced, but a corset nonetheless.

She had a bruise blooming on her cheekbone where she had run into the hilt of Torin's practice blade, while dodging a grab from her left hand. She pressed on it with her fingertips, the sharp jab of pain grounding her nervous energy. She grinned remembering how Amelia had groaned and fussed when she realized all the powders in the world would not conceal it.

She peaked around the door into the great hall and her heartbeat quickened. So many people! So many men, and she was expected to dance with them all! She began to back away, brimming with thoughts of running to the forest, sleeping in a cave, grabbing a horse from the stable and riding as fast as she could through the night. She would flee anywhere as long as it was far from here. She felt a grip on her elbow and whirled, neatly dislodging her arm from her assailant.

Only to find Hildegard, hands up in surrender, in full courtly attire.

"Oh-ho!" Marri exclaimed, "Look at you! Are you posing as a lord now, vying for my hand as well?"

Hilde's face turned red and she rolled her eyes at the younger woman. "Don't be stupid. The Queen knew you'd need some handling and I couldn't exactly attend a ball in my practice leathers, could I?"

"Need handling, do I?" Marri exclaimed, incensed.

"Ha! Marriander, who do you think you're talking to? I can see it in your eyes. If I hadn't found you just now you'd be halfway to the Other Kingdom before the first reel!"

"I doubt I'd have made it past the stables, actually, let alone the Other Kingdom," Marri grumbled.

Briefly she wished she knew where to find entrance to that land, but no one knew exactly where it lay and all the directions she had ever come across where maddeningly vague. Ride west so fast that you never let the setting sun slip past the horizon. Ride north until the night is absolute and the day is forever absent, and other such impossible nonsense.

Hilde grinned and offered her arm. "Are you ready for your ball, my Princess?"

Marri groaned, "Spare me, please! Knock me over the head and throw me into the river in a sack, or sell me to the high mountain trolls. Anything would be preferable to this."

Large, rough hands tenderly cupped her face, forcing her to look into Hilde's grey eyes. "Marri, my heart, you will get through this. I do not pretend to know the outcome, but I do know that you are on your path, love, and you must follow it to its conclusion. There are no detours. You must be brave and trust that things will turn out right.

Trust that there is a way for you to do your duty by the kingdom and stay true to your desires walking the same path. You will be Queen one day, and that will make things both simpler for you and much more complicated. Now, I ask you again, Princess, are you ready for your ball?"

The evening proceeded in a blur. Marri produced a strained smile and managed not to scream in the face of every young man she was forced to dance with. She searched periodically for Torin but saw her nowhere.

Towards the end of the evening she managed to duck behind one of the larger statues and hide in its shadow. She leaned her forehead against the cool marble and closed her eyes.

An arm snaked itself around her waist and she stiffened, preparing to fight.

"Shhh," a voice by her ear, "Its only me."

She opened her eyes to find Torin's brown ones right in front of her, deep and dark like woodland pools. The Lord's lips were inches from her own, so close she could taste her breath, smoky and sweet by turns.

"Enjoying your evening, then?" Torin asked, surprising a small laugh from Marri. "Care to duck out?"

"I would love to, but there are guards in the form of my friends and family set to watch for my escape, far more fearsome than a legion of enemy warriors!" A few exasperated tears slid down Marri's face. Torin's thumb brushed at them. She squinted through shadow at her bruised cheek.

"Oh, did I give you that?" She grimaced.

"Nothing a little arnica poultice won't take care of," Marri said off handedly, leaning into the caress like a cat.

"You don't mind a little pain, do you?" Torin's voice was soft and inexplicably sent shivers down Marri's spine.

"No," she replied, heat rising up her neck to her face, "I don't."

Torin shook herself, as though freeing herself from a trance, and said, "I know a way. It's right behind this statue. I thought that was why you ducked back here." She reached her hand into a crevice and a small panel in the wall opened, just wide enough for them to slip through.

Marri was astonished. She had spent years of her childhood scouring the castle for its secrets and thought she knew all of them. As Torin slipped through into the dark passageway, Marri grabbed her arm.

"Who are you?" She asked.

"Torin of Surrain," she replied, "at your service."

The door closed behind them and they were in total darkness. It was so absolute that Marri gasped, feeling dizzy, unmoored. And then, just as suddenly, there was a blaze of light. Torin held a lit torch in front of them, illuminating a rough-hewn passage stretching before them.

"Where did that torch come from? How did you know this passage was here?" Marri felt on the verge of a tantrum.

"I have a talent for finding hidden ways," was her enigmatic reply, her eyes glinting strangely in the shadow. "Come on, this passage leads to a closet in a room three doors down from your chambers."

Emerging from the room, they peered into the hallway but all was clear. The servants had been given the night off to celebrate in the village and no one was about.

"They will come looking for me soon," Marri said.

"Where will they look first?"

"The training yard, most likely, and the stables after that. They might even search the woods." She spared a moment to feel sorry for Hilde and the tongue-lashing she would receive from the Queen as soon as she was found missing.

"I didn't think you were the kind of princess to retreat to her chambers. We should have some time then."

Once in her bedroom Marri started pacing, wanting to rip the formal garb from her body, but terribly conscious of Torin's gaze. She leaned against the door, arms crossed over her chest, watching Marri pace.

"So what's the problem then? Why are you so upset?" she finally asked.

"Oh, I don't know," Marri hissed, "Maybe it's the fifty men panting at my skirts, expecting me to share my bed and the rest of my days with them!"

"Oh, they're not that bad. Some of them are halfway decent lads. And I'm sure any number of them would make fantastic bedfellows."

"You're laughing at me!" Marriander shrieked. "It isn't as if you have to deal with every lord in the land vying to get between your legs!" She ripped at her hair, scattering pins and unwinding the heavy coils of her tresses. "If this was all that stood in my way I would gladly cut my hair as short as you and Hilde's! I would don riding leathers everyday if it would make them leave me in peace. I have tried that, and it makes no difference!"

"What is it that you want, Marriander?" Torin asked in her soft, deep voice. She pushed herself off of the door and walked toward her.

"To be free of my life," Marri exclaimed, throwing her hands in the air.

There was a flash of a blade in Torin's hand.

"What are you doing?" Marri asked, backing away.

"I'm going to free you from your life," Torin said with her crooked grin. "For the evening anyway."

Marriander felt uncertain. The ins and outs of disarming an assailant with a dagger had been one of her first lessons with Hilde, but she was curious to see where this was going.

Torin made a sudden move and pressed herself against Marri's body. She tried to widen the distance between them, but Torin placed her booted foot behind her slippered one and she crashed to the floor, knocking her head painfully on the flagstones. Torin dropped to the floor on top of her. Marri found Torin's weight both menacing and strangely comforting.

"Trust me," Torin whispered in her ear, her lips soft and not unpleasantly moist against her neck.

The blade slipped under the edge of her bodice and the fine material parted easily along its sharp edge. Marriander lay still as her outer garments were dissected slowly and methodically. By the time her under garments were exposed, her breast was heaving and she was feeling light headed, both from her fall and the powerful lust riding the blood through her veins.

Torin rolled her over and slid the blade under her corset stays.

One by one she cut the laces, each easing the flow of air and blood. Finally the corset parted, revealing the full expanse of Marri's back. She felt the blade's edge, lightly traced over the surface of her skin, and it awoke in her a fierce desire to feel the prick of its tip passing into her flesh.

She wiggled beneath Torin's weight, arched her back to increase the pressure of the knife.

"Shhh, lie still," Torin said, her hand coming to rest on the back of Marri's neck. Her palm was blazing hot, uncomfortably so. "What is it that you want, Marriander?"

"I want to feel it," she gasped.

"Feel what, exactly?"

Embarrassment pulsed hot to her cheeks, "The blade, damn you! I want to feel the blade bite my flesh, I want to bleed from it!"

"Now, now, Princess," Torin's hand gripped a hunk of tangled locks and wrenched her head off the floor. "Do you take me for one of your servants? Or perhaps you mistake me for Hildegard, who seems to have far more tolerance for your brattishness and petulance? I am not so lenient."

Bringing her knee to the small of her back, Torin held Marri's hands painfully behind her back and efficiently tied them together with strips of fabric from her dress. She then flipped her over, exposing her breasts as her torso arched up over the top of her bound hands.

Torin's hands were everywhere and devilishly hot, pinching her nipples, slapping her breasts and her face, so hard she saw stars. Marriander was dizzy with heat and lust and pain.

"Please," she whispered.

Torin stopped her assault. "What was that you said?"

"Please, Torin."

"Please, what? What is it that you would like me to do, Princess?"

Marriander's face turned hot. The fact of the matter was, she wasn't quite sure what she was asking for. She was not a complete innocent, but she had been sheltered enough that there had been few dalliances in her life thus far, and none of those fumblings had prepared her for whatever this was taking place between her and Torin.

"Would you like me to stop?" Torin asked softly.

"No, please, don't stop," Marri begged, tears leaking from her eyes.

"I like it when you're polite," Torin said, stroking her cheek. "Would you like me to keep hurting you?"

Marri shut her eyes. "Yes," she whispered. "Please." Her eyes flew back open. "But, Torin," she hesitated, "would you use your blade? Please?"

Torin smiled, "Yes, Princess, I will."

The tip was hot when it touched the skin of her breast, and its bite made Marri's body shiver all over. She looked down to see the shallow trench slowly fill with her blood, spilling over and dripping down her ribcage. Another appeared along side it, and another, until her breasts where decorated with crimson rays, brimming over.

Torin lowered her head and licked the cut flesh, sucking the blood from the wounds and groaning deep in her chest. Marri was frenzied, her body bucking wildly, trying to get as much of her lover as she could with her arms trapped under her body as they were. She imagined them free, pulling Torin to her, raking her nails down the lordling's back.

"Please, Torin, please!" Torin lifted her mouth from Marri's swollen nipple, eyes smoldering, her face covered in scarlet. "I need you."

Torin's blazing hands reached for Marri's linen underskirt, shoving it aside and spreading her legs wide. Her fingertips slipped between the folds of her nether lips and found her sodden and swollen. Marri writhed, thrusting herself against Torin's burning fingers. They slipped inside of her, stretching her open and feeling like a brand. Marri screamed, slamming her head against the stones of the floor. Her body was on fire, her blood replaced with molten flame. Pain and the most tormenting pleasure that she had ever experienced fought along her nerves. Blackness threatened to swallow her vision as the overwhelming sensations emanating from Torin's fingers boiled deep inside her. Her body was seized by powerful convulsions and she arched into her lover, giving herself over. Finally her muscles relaxed one by one and she lay still and exhausted on the stones.

Torin stroked her face, eyes flashing in the candlelight. There was something strange about them. They were luminous, like glowing embers. And why, in the Goddess's name, was her skin so blisteringly hot?

"Who are you?" Marriander asked for the third time, with the first stirrings of real fear.

"Torin of the Other Kingdom, at your service," she replied, her voice low and resonant.

"The Other Kingdom! You said you were from Surrain!"

"Yes, well. I lied."

"*What* are you?"

"A fire mage," she mumbled. "An apprentice, anyway. Roll

over, I need to get those bindings off you before you lose circulation."

Marri complied, feeling the knife slice through the strips of fabric. She righted herself and scooted away from Torin, rubbing the feeling back into her wrists and glaring at her suspiciously.

"Why didn't you just tell me? We've had delegations from the Other Kingdom before."

"Not for the last hundred and fifty years," Torin replied, running a hand distractedly through her hair. "Anyway, it's complicated."

Marri crossed her arms over her naked, blood-streaked breasts and said, "Explain it to me then."

"Can we sit on your bed? These flag stones are uncomfortable." Torin's request surprised Marri, but she rose and flung her half naked length unselfconsciously onto the bed. She propped her arm underneath her head. The tug of gravity on her breasts opened her cuts, sending thrills of pain along her nerves.

Torin's eyes flashed at her as she eased onto the bed. "You are stunningly beautiful, you know."

Marri snorted, "Do you honestly think you can distract me with flattery?"

"No, but it bears saying regardless. You are lovely; you glow like a lantern. I've been half in love with you ever since the first time I saw you. I believe you were 12 at the time."

Marri shot up. "What is this?" her voice was cold with intensity.

Torin held up her hand in supplication. "Let me speak Marriander. The first time I saw you, you were sparring with Hildegard in a clearing in the great wood. I shouldn't have been there.

I had slipped out of classes with Master that day, restless for adventure. I found the nearest door to this realm, in the side of a large oak on the grounds of my school."

"You came here through a tree?" Marri interrupted, incredulous. In all of her readings on how to gain entrance to the Other Kingdom, doorways in trees had never been mentioned.

Torin sighed. "The door appears at certain times. When the sun rises and the rays reach the bark through the neighboring trees, a crevice appears, just large enough to slip through. I found it when I was exploring one morning. I told you, I am good at finding hidden ways. Shall I continue?"

"Yes, please."

Torin smiled. "I do love it when you are polite," she said, tracing a fingertip along her clavicle and down toward her breast.

Marri shivered. "Please continue and please stop trying to distract me. Please," she said through gritted teeth.

Torin chuckled, then quickly sobered as her thoughts returned to her story. "The portals are ever shifting; you can never be sure where they will come out exactly. This particular time, I came out in your great wood. I exited into the shadow of a clearing where a young girl and an older, much larger warrior were doing battle. I was about run in and even the odds when I heard you laugh, and saw that what I had taken for swords were actually wooden practice blades."

Torin paused, her gaze turning soft and far away. "You were so full of joy. Every part of your being was engaged in that fight. It was beautiful to behold, I had never seen anything like it."

"Do women not fight in your world?"

"Some do. Technically, I'm one of them if you recall." She

placed her hot palm on Marri's waist and leaned in to nuzzle her ear.

Marri gasped and pushed her away. "Okay, that explains how you fist saw me. What brings you here, now?"

"That wasn't the only time I've seen you. There were others, throughout the years. As I told you, I was half in love and you were never far from my thoughts. Several months ago, I was exploring south of your kingdom and came upon the proclamation calling for any of royal blood to come and plead their suit for your hand. I felt crazed thinking of you marrying some noble. You were mine, in my mind anyway, had always been destined to be mine. So I decided to come and claim you." Torin had been creeping ever closer during this confession and she ended with teeth sinking gently into Marriander's neck.

"Claim me, would you?" said Marri, without much sting, as she melted into Torin's embrace. She knew there was much of the story that had been left out and she resolved to pry it from the lordling at a later date. Piece by piece, if she had to.

"Yes," Torin replied, raising her head and staring into Marri's eyes, "I would. Will you have me?"

Rock Palace

I'd been contemplating the pros and cons of taking Lilly to visit the farm for a while. It was one of those decisions that could make or break a thing and it took awhile for me to stop shying away from the risk. It was half way through June before I faced those fears and realized waiting wasn't doing me a bit of good.

I had spent huge chunks of my childhood on that farm, raised by my grandma. She was still strong as an ox, but she was getting up there in age. It had been awhile since small farms had made much of a living in those parts. She had downscaled, sold the dairy cows her folks had tended decades before, all but a couple sweet tempered jerseys. She had a small nest egg, and mostly she farmed for herself, family, and immediate neighbors.

She liked to take vacations every now and then, usually into town to stay with my aunt, giving her a break from tending goats, chickens, cows, and vegetables. She had a promise from me that I would keep the farm running when she was gone, both when she was in town and when she "finally passed over", as she put it. It was a promise I meant to keep.

Gram would be taking off this particular weekend to see a play she had tickets for and I'd be watching the farm. I wanted to take Lilly out there with me, which wasn't a move I'd usually make while courting a girl.

Most of my life I had been simultaneously proud and ashamed of where I came from. When your identities are many, it sometimes leaves you feeling stranded in the middle of a busy intersection, not knowing which way to take to find your home. Sometimes you pick one at the expense of the others in order to find a place to fit, a community. My queerness had taken precedence awhile back, which did not change the fact that I was rural and poor living in the city. I was surrounded by downwardly mobile queers from the suburbs and I passed as one of them, leaving other parts of me lonely and invisible.

You leave the place you were raised and sometimes you leave your context. I had tried to build myself another one, but it was full of holes, a sinking ship. Having just turned 30 I was feeling that post Saturn return urge to cut through the bullshit and clarify who my people were, get down to the business of following my heart and my gut. Just fucking do it.

I was tired of renting, tired of slum lords and shitty apartments that I worked so hard to make decent while paying someone else's mortgage. I wanted to settle and I wanted to find folks who wanted to settle with me. Among them, I was hoping to find a girl to cuddle up against on those brutal winter nights when the walls of the old farmhouse felt like they were made of tissue paper.

For years, I had made it a habit of falling for high femmes who tended to scream at the sight of insects, didn't own shoes that would hold up on gravel, and who only liked getting dirty in the bedroom. Those women were strong, brilliant people, but there were always parts of my life I just could not share with them.

Lilly was different. Being also from a rural, working background she made me feel at home in a way I hadn't even realized I'd been missing until I met her. It stirred things up, got me thinking about the slow building pressure I'd been sensing in my life. She was like vinegar, my thoughts the baking soda, turning the inside of my brain into some volcano in a sixth grader's science fair.

She was sweet and grounded and shockingly honest. She had sharp insight and more energy than anyone I had ever met. She laughed at me even when I wasn't trying to be funny and instead of feeling embarrassed about this I felt strangely proud.

It was silly, this lingering apprehension, but I couldn't seem to shake it. The farm had always been a safe haven for me and I protected it like my heart.

She seemed genuinely excited though, when I asked her to go out there with me.

"Taylor! I love goats! I always wanted some growing up, but my parents never went for it. Can I milk them?" She bubbled over, throwing her arms around me and pressing herself against me in a way that made me secretly frantic.

Lilly was almost as tall as my 5'10". She had a body that was made up of one luscious curve after another. Awe inspiring. She was a big girl and she was not ashamed of it. I embarrassed myself regularly, comparing her to certain Divinity in my head.

"Sure sweets, you can have your pick of farm chores." I said, wrapping my arms around her waist and burying my nose in her brown curls. Anything, this girl could have anything she wanted from me.

The summer started off hot that year and the cut off jean shorts Lilly was wearing when I picked her up were going to drive me crazy all day. She was carrying a bag with her, knitting needles sticking out the top. She always brought some kind of project with her, wherever she went, to keep her hands busy.

"I'm wearing the bikini I knit last week under this, so I hope you have a swimming hole somewhere on this farm."

I swallowed convulsively, "You bet, sugar. There's a great one not too far from the house."

She grabbed her needles and started knitting as I backed out of her driveway. "I brought sandwiches if you're hungry. Cheese and sprouts."

Lilly was raised by hippies. The sandwiches were probably made on home baked whole wheat bread. I was raised with bologna on white bread with my dad, but had been spoiled by my grandma's complex and nutritious food.

The farm was about an hour from Lilly's house. I tried to keep my mind on the road and the pleasant conversation Lilly was trying to make. I tried to stop staring at the swell of her breasts exposed by the low cut of her tank top, something I couldn't help but notice every time I glanced over at her. This was going to come to a head soon; that was obvious. The realization filled me with a restless tension, made the floor of my stomach drop about two feet.

It hadn't rained in the last week and the final stretch of dirt road was so dry that we had to roll up the windows to block out clouds of dust. The air was hot, heavy with humidity. We were both sticky with sweat, our skin gritty by the time we pulled up to the farmhouse.

Lilly jumped out of the truck right away, this look of awe on her beautiful face. Turning to me she said, "Taylor, it's gorgeous! You didn't tell me."

I'll admit, early summer is a good time on the farm. Something about the light and the new green of everything, all the imperfections of the old buildings get smoothed out. The flowerbeds and the vegetable gardens haven't been completely taken over by weeds yet, and the grass is still pretty low. Come back in August and this place is a fucking jungle.

It was my home for much of my life and would be again. I put as much of my energy and heart into it as I could manage with my busy days. I loved it like no other place, but I hadn't thought to describe it to this girl as beautiful. I was gratified by her admiration so deeply, it just shed more light on how anxious I'd been about her reaction to the place.

I grinned at her, letting my heart loosen up in a different way. I filled with relief as that tight place eased inside me.

She grinned back at me, closed the distance between us and placed her lips on my dusty cheek.

I took a deep breath. I reminded myself that it's never good to rush these things. We had two whole days together out here. Alone. I didn't have to fuck this girl in the driveway the first five minutes of our stay.

I brushed some stray hair behind her ear. "You really like it, princess?"

"I love it. It feels amazing here." She looked over her shoulder at the house and I leaned in, kissed the hollow between neck and jaw. I allowed myself that much.

I cleared the dust and tension from my throat and said, "Lilly, you want to catch that swim now? There's nothing for us to really do until dusk, unless you want to weed Gram's perennial beds."

She giggled and ran her fingers over the back of my neck, turning eyes on me that made my center melt like butter on a griddle. She said, "I'd love to go for a swim."

The path to the swim hole had been cleared recently. I hadn't gotten around to it this year, so I figured maybe my Aunt's husband had been out here. He was a good guy and tried to help Gram out as much as he had time for.

It wasn't far to the river, but our sweat was running freely by the time we reached the bend that formed the pool just big enough for a satisfying dip. I started stripping off my jeans and T-shirt, feeling self-conscious despite the boxer briefs and tank top I had on underneath. Lilly, on the other hand, couldn't get out of her clothes fast enough and the bikini she wore was just a little bit more than a formality. She strode into the water, yelping at the cold, and dunked under at the deepest point. I followed more slowly, letting myself acclimate. She swam circles around me like a selkie, giggling and splashing at me until I dove at her, pulling her down into the water with me. We surfaced, sputtering.

Her arms wrapped around me, her warm mammalian body pressed against mine in the cold water. She smelled so good, traces of vanilla, stream water and summer skin. I wanted to lay her down, stretch her out and touch all that exposed flesh.

I remembered a place I used to hide as a kid, a place of rock and sky and soft moss. I had spent a lot of my turbulent adolescence hiding out there, reading sci-fi novels, thinking and crying when shit got bad. I learned to jerk off there, reading old smutty paperbacks I found in my dad's garage. The give of the moss under my ass and the rock rough against my back created an intense and irresistible contrast. It was my palace, my fortress, whatever I needed. I had never even thought to share that spot with anyone.

"I want to take you someplace." I said, angling our bodies toward land, forging a smooth passage through water.

136

I watched her pull herself out of the water, watched her body rejoin gravity, that awkward moment of heavy disorientation. Her bikini bottoms sagged around her curves, saturated with water, and she pulled at them, giggling self-consciously.

"I haven't quite figured that part out yet," she said, smiling back at me in this way I felt in my gut.

The opening to my old hideout looked dank and cramped and shadowed in a way that embarrassed me, made me wonder what had possessed me to bring a girl here.

"I haven't been here in a while, maybe we should forget it," I said, scratching the back of my head.

"It's through here?" Her voice was bubbly, up for anything. She got down on her hands and knees, started wiggling through the opening. My face heated up watching her from behind, ass so sexy, her back arched as she crawled through the small space in the rock. I worried about her knees. Five seconds and she was out of sight, just her toes visible in the dappled sunlight on the other side.

"Holy shit, this is beautiful!"

I was way smaller the last time I had come here, but I crouched down and crawled through, the rock hard and rough under my weight.

The space opened up, a small chamber carpeted in soft, thick moss. The walls were formed by massive granite boulders, smoothed down and spit out by long ago glaciers. They clustered together against the hill to hide this space, an old secret privacy. The sky was an intense blue above us, small shreds of sunlight filtering down through the trees on the hillside. She was staring around in wonder, her knees pressing into the damp, moss covered earth. She sat down, arranged herself, and looked over at me.

"So, how many girls have you brought here?" Her head cocked, smiling in this way that said she was a good sport but I'd better be careful answering.

"I've never brought a girl here." I said. "The girls I've dated are too city to appreciate this."

She looked away, her face a shutter slowly closing.

"I'm not really your type, am I," she said, like she was sad, but also resigned.

I was baffled. I looked at her, her body so ripe and luscious that her handmade bikini didn't even begin to contain it. I felt a pain in my heart, a hairline fracture, watching this girl lose her confidence. She was sitting there in a swim suit she had been taught her whole life she did not have a right to wear and she looked so fucking beautiful I thought I might hyperventilate or dissolve if I didn't get my hands on her soon. How could she possibly not be aware of her effect on me?

"You are exactly my type. I've just never met anyone like you before."

She looked at me, curiously. "Ditto," she said, and I laughed, because that's always what the emotionally stunted guy says in the movies after the girl says 'I love you'. "No, I mean it. That's kind of how I feel about you too."

She was serious; I saw it in the crease forming on her brow. "Come here," she said. All her insecurity gone, her body opened up like an invitation.

Her feet were closest to me so I went for those first, raising her toes to my lips. Her giggles turned to a low moan as I ran my tongue over her instep.

"Taylor, come *here*."

She grabbed me, and lying back, pulled me to her, water logged clothing pressing together between us. Her mouth found mine and I couldn't remember feeling anything more soft than my bottom lip between hers, her skin under my hands, her body pressed underneath me.

It was the easiest thing in the world to slip her breasts from her bikini top and slip her nipple into my mouth. She was so generous with her response, with her body. It made my heart ache in my chest the way she opened herself to me. The way she gave me access. It made me painfully hard the way her body moved in waves under me, the way she sighed and moaned, arched her back and cried out when my teeth found her neck.

I wanted to please her until there was no question in her mind that she was a goddess, no question that she deserved every second of pleasure I could give her. The beast in me wanted to get rough with her, sink my teeth into that luscious flesh and watch the colors bloom under her skin. I wanted to mark her, make her irrevocably mine.

Words fell from our mouths in clusters between kisses.

You feel so good, I've wanted this for so long, I love your body, you are so fucking beautiful, I love the weight of you on top of me, yes, please, just like that, yes.

It felt ridiculously good to hear the word 'baby' come out of her mouth, all soft and rolling off her tongue, and know she was talking to me. It felt ridiculously good to slip my fingers between her legs and into all that hot wetness, watching her eyes roll back and her limbs go weak as I slid in and out of her. I found a spot inside her and when I stroked it at the right angle the most glorious sounds came out of her mouth. I wanted to make her come with a fierceness that surprised me, making all my muscles tense and my teeth close on her neck a bit harder than I meant to.

With a sharp cry, she convulsed around my fingers, spurts of her come splashing her thighs and soaking into the moss. I kissed away the pain I had caused, held her until the convulsions stopped and she came back to herself. Slowly she opened her eyes and looked into mine, the light and shadow from the leaves above playing on her beautiful face.

"I'm so glad it's you," she mumbled and pulled my lips down to hers.

Even with all the heat our bodies generated, the combination of the lengthening shadows and our wet clothing had us shivering and covered in goose flesh before long. We crawled from our hide away searching for some afternoon sun. We found a nice patch stretching across the bed in the guest room and discovered just how squeaky one of those old brass bed frames can be. I am truly surprised we didn't break the thing, and that we haven't since.

It was dark before we drug ourselves to the kitchen, starving. Lilly was adorable in one of my button-ups, only the middle two buttons fastened, the fabric straining against the gorgeous abundance of her chest.

There was all the expected awkwardness of sharing a kitchen for the first time with someone you are newly in love with. Despite the fact that the kitchen is large with plenty of counter space I couldn't seem to be anywhere but right on top of her. We were lightheaded from sex hormones and lack of food, and we could barely keep our hands off each other long enough to produce anything edible. Finally,

Lilly kicked me out to milk the goats and in the absence of my distractions conjured up some culinary magic.

Eating that first meal together, I remember wondering how each bite of food could possibly make it past the swollen mass my heart had become, and how the hell I was going to convince this woman to marry me and start some crazy family with me in a falling-down farmhouse in the middle of nowhere.

It was a lot easier than I thought it would be, but that's a different story.

Acknowledgements

With deepest gratitude I thank everyone who participated in bringing this book to life.

To Sage and Anna for being my proofreaders, and for all the support and words of encouragement. To Dara for the cover photos, for being an amazing director, and for opening the shoot up beyond my limited imagination. To C and T for being my models, for trekking around the woods in three and a half inch heels, and for getting over self consciousness enough to get some amazing shots. To Sacchi, Anna, Sassafras, and Maggie for writing blurbs, thank you!

Thanks to everyone from the Queer Smut Writers group back in the day, for your feedback, support, and believing in my writing, not to mention the flowers (Ireney). Thanks to Maggie and Johnny Blazes for encouraging me to put out a collection of my stories. To my sister for suggesting I get fancy and self publish, for last minute formatting help, and for supporting me all the time in all of my projects! Thanks to Carolyn, Lani, Katie, tk, Lisabeth, Ada, Silke, Shoogie, Anna Ruby, and everyone else who has let me read them various versions of my stories and given me feedback. To Lauren and Vanessa for encouraging me to fundraise, and for listening and being excited for this book.

I am so blessed and grateful to have so much love and support.

www.ingramcontent.com/pod-product-compliance
Lightning Source LLC
Chambersburg PA
CBHW020236290526
45784CB00003B/1002